National Defense Research Institute

THE INFORMATION REVOLUTION IN THE MIDDLE EAST AND NORTH AFRICA

Grey E. Burkhart

Susan Older

RAND

Prepared for the
National Intelligence Council

The research described in this report was sponsored by the Office of the Secretary of Defense (OSD). The research was conducted in RAND's National Defense Research Institute, a federally funded research and development center supported by the OSD, the Joint Staff, the unified commands, and the defense agencies under Contract DASW01-01-C-0004.

Library of Congress Cataloging-in-Publication Data

Burkhart, Grey E.
    The information revolution in the Middle East and North Africa : MR-1653 /
Grey E. Burkhart, Susan Older.
        p. cm.
    Includes bibliographical references.
    ISBN 0-8330-3323-9 (pbk.)
        1. Information technology—Economic aspects—Middle East. 2. Information
technology—Economic aspects—Africa, North. 3. Information technology—Social
aspects—Middle East. 4. Information technology—Social aspects—Africa, North.
5. Information technology—Government policy—Middle East. 6. Information
technology—Government policy—Africa, North. 7. Globalization. I. Older, Susan.
II.Title.

HC415.15.Z9I552 2003
303.48'33'0956—dc21

                                                                                    2002154572

RAND is a nonprofit institution that helps improve policy and decisionmaking through research and analysis. RAND® is a registered trademark. RAND's publications do not necessarily reflect the opinions or policies of its research sponsors.

Published 2003 by RAND
1700 Main Street, P.O. Box 2138, Santa Monica, CA 90407-2138
1200 South Hayes Street, Arlington, VA 22202-5050
201 North Craig Street, Suite 202, Pittsburgh, PA 15213-1516
RAND URL: http://www.rand.org/
To order RAND documents or to obtain additional information,
contact Distribution Services: Telephone: (310) 451-7002;
Fax: (310) 451-6915; Email: order@rand.org

RAND is conducting a multiyear effort, sponsored by the National Intelligence Council (NIC), to explore the future of the information revolution throughout the world.[1] This is a multidisciplinary effort with a broad range of participants from both inside and outside of RAND, with an overarching goal of mapping the likely future of the global information revolution over the next one to two decades.

This effort has included a series of international conferences on specific aspects of the information revolution, involving experts in various relevant areas. The proceedings of these conferences have been documented in the following RAND publications:

Richard O. Hundley, Robert H. Anderson, Tora K. Bikson, James A. Dewar, Jerrold Green, Martin Libicki, and C. Richard Neu, *The Global Course of the Information Revolution: Political, Economic, and Social Consequences: Proceedings of an International Conference*, Santa Monica, Calif.: RAND, CF-154-NIC, 2000.

Robert H. Anderson, Philip S. Anton, Steven K. Bankes, Tora K. Bikson, Jonathan Caulkins, Peter J. Denning, James A. Dewar, Richard O. Hundley, and C. Richard Neu, *The Global Course of the Information Revolution: Technology Trends: Proceedings of an International Conference*, Santa Monica, Calif.: RAND, CF-157-NIC, 2000.

---

[1]This effort is being carried out in support of the Information Revolution initiative of the DCI's Strategic Estimates Program.

Gregory F. Treverton and Lee Mizell, *The Future of the Information Revolution in Latin America: Proceedings of an International Conference,* Santa Monica, Calif.: RAND, CF-166-1-NIC, 2001.

Richard O. Hundley, Robert H. Anderson, Tora K. Bikson, Maarten Botterman, Jonathan Cave, C. Richard Neu, Michelle Norgat,e and Renée Cordes, *The Future of the Information Revolution in Europe: Proceedings of an International Conference,* Santa Monica, Calif.: RAND, CF-172-NIC, 2001.

In addition to these international conferences, in-depth studies have been conducted on selected subjects. This publication reports the results of one of those studies, on the likely course of the information revolution in the Middle East and North Africa over the next five to 10 years. Key questions addressed in this report include the extent to which the information revolution has taken hold in this region in general, the variations between individual countries, and prospects for further information technology (IT)-related developments in the region.

Regarding the authors: Grey Burkhart is an analyst based in Washington, D.C., and Susan Older is a journalist and president of Real World Media, based in New York City. They both have extensive experience in the Middle East. They carried out this study while working under contract to RAND.

This research was sponsored by the National Intelligence Council and monitored by the National Intelligence Officer (NIO) for Science and Technology. It was conducted by the Acquisition and Technology Policy Center of RAND's National Defense Research Institute (NDRI). NDRI is a federally funded research and development center sponsored by the Office of the Secretary of Defense, the Joint Staff, the defense agencies, and the unified commands.

CONTENTS

TABLES

Most of the countries of the Middle East and North Africa (MENA) show no signs of impending information revolutions (IRs). The exceptions are the only democracies in the region: Israel and Turkey.[2] The proliferation and ever-more-sophisticated employment of information and communication technologies (ICTs) are critically dependent upon economic factors and the nature of the government and its role in ICT development. Except for Israel and Turkey, every other country in the region is deficient in necessary economic factors or government participation; several, such as Algeria and Yemen, are deficient in both.

While the factors underpinning an information revolution are many, complex, and interrelated, three aspects are cause for immediate concern with respect to MENA countries:

- The likelihood that most of the region's countries will miss the information revolution altogether, while others experience a belated "information evolution." This will increase the development gap between MENA and Organization of Economic Cooperation and Development (OECD) countries.

---

[2]Israel and Turkey will not be examined in detail in this report, and are mentioned generally as exceptions to regional norms. Israel can almost be said not to be a Middle Eastern country except for geography, which creates other problems for that state. Although a country of Muslims, Turkey is not an Islamic state by any metric; it is officially and aggressively secular. While Turkey shares in some of the information-revolution concerns of the region, its development process and prospects are unique and merit detailed examination elsewhere.

- The generally low level of ICT penetration in most of the region's countries, independent of any consideration of an information revolution. This, too, will exacerbate the gap between MENA countries and the modern world.

- The irregular pattern of ICT diffusion and use, irrespective of the magnitude of ICT, favoring the wealthy and privileged. This pattern will increase the standard of living and opportunity gaps between the richest and poorest sectors of MENA societies, resulting in continued unrest—including armed rebellion and the export of terrorism—and justification for a government's strict controls, which contributed to the problem in the first place.

Furthermore, the development of a technical industrial or service sector in particular and ICT issues in general are not front-burner issues in most MENA countries; the United Arab Emirates (UAE) may be the only exception. More basic infrastructure issues—particularly ground-transport networks, electrical-power generation and distribution, and the availability, extent, and exploitability of water supplies—occupy the time, attention, and funds of all MENA countries, even the wealthiest. Unlike in other developing regions, hunger and disease are not major problems in MENA. However, these countries are experiencing the same population pressures arising from high birth rates, decreasing infant mortality, and extended life expectancy.

GLOBALIZATION

Global economic integration is happening, whether developing countries are ready for it or not. This alone represents an information revolution of sorts in countries with closed and tightly controlled financial systems, most notably Syria and pre-war Iraq. (The latter is in no danger from globalization or an information revolution in the foreseeable future.) All MENA countries rely heavily on exports for their national budgets, and most import food and manufactured goods extensively, especially industrial and consumer durables. Trade today is facilitated by electronic ordering and funds transfers, both of which are difficult—in some cases illegal—in the face of ICT underdevelopment. Most central banks in the region are connected via the SWIFT financial settlement network, but actual inbound funds transfers to individuals and businesses can still take weeks and be essentially untrackable while in progress. E-mail is proliferating, but Telex remains an important means of communication.

Global social familiarization, if not integration, is also proceeding apace. It is based on the rapid proliferation over the past decade of satellite television distribution. In countries with poor IT development, extensive dispersed rural populations, and notable illiteracy levels, the television set is the preferred tool for sharing information. Regional governments have tightly controlled television broadcasting since its inception, using this tool to attract viewers through entertainment and to shape their thinking through news and information programming. They have not been particularly successful on either score. Entertainment-seeking people risked arrest and fines to erect satellite television dishes. With the advent of broadcasting in the Ku-band, which allows the use of a significantly smaller antenna dish, satellite antennas sprouted from roofs like mushrooms, a phenomenon that was more pronounced in the poorer districts. People thus got their first extensive look at Western culture and had several sources of news to choose from. In both cases, this was not seen as a universal good, even by the viewing population. BBC was interesting when it was new, but over time MENA populations have begun to wonder whether it was any more free from distortions than their local news. The Discovery Channel is one of the few enduring hits.

Religious, cultural, and, especially, security authorities viewed the proliferation of satellite television as cultural competition, a competition that they dare not lose. Some governments retreated into their preferred mode and prohibited the reception of satellite television except by permit (usually reserved for government information agencies and the elite). None was successful. Every country in the region, however, launched its own satellite television broadcasts in an attempt at cultural "co-opetition." The Iranian authorities went so far as to lease transponder bandwidth for broadcasts to Europe in the stated belief that Persian culture would be seen by Europeans to be superior to their own. That did not work. But what has happened is that the population of the region is now routinely exposed to the propaganda and interpretations of all regional governments. The most noted example is Qatar's controversial Al-Jazeera network, only one of more than twenty "local" channels that have more subtle social effects.

GOVERNANCE

None of the region's governments, excepting Israel and Turkey, has been installed as the result of what the United States considers "free and fair" elections. To the extent that they lack legitimacy to varying degrees, these governments maintain strong central control over most aspects of life and commerce. Besides being necessary, from the government's point of view, rule by a strong central leader or group is a cultural norm in most of these societies.

Control of information flows is central to maintaining control over the populace, and is also central to commercial practices. So, technology that speeds and broadens the dissemination of information can counter the government's needs. As each new technology appeared (e.g., the telephone, radio, television, and now the Internet), the authorities came to terms with it and adapted the technology to their own purposes. Telephones not only allowed people to talk to one another at a distance, but provided the government the potential to listen in on conversations that otherwise might have taken place in person and been less susceptible to eavesdropping. Radio and television became propaganda and socialization tools.[3] So, too, are the governments coming to terms with the Internet. But just as the tool is more complicated than its predecessors, so, too, is it more difficult to harness effectively. But that has not stopped any government in the region from trying.

With respect to the information revolution in general, and the Internet in particular, MENA countries can be grouped into three categories: Fearful, desiring the "Best of Both," or Driven.

The Fearful countries include Algeria, Iraq, Libya, and Syria, countries that have limited Internet connectivity or that have prohibited it altogether. They would rather forgo the potential benefits in order to ensure they avoid any negative consequences of joining the networked world. Syria recently made some cautious steps, and Libya is testing the waters also.

---

[3]To this day, Iraqis without access to outside information believe that Iraq won the 1991 war with the U.S.–led coalition.

The "Best of Both" countries are Iran, Saudi Arabia, Tunisia, and the UAE, each of which has tried to develop a tightly controlled domestic Internet network that will enable them to reap benefits in commerce, academia, and government while keeping a close watch of and maintaining strict limits on what can and cannot be done and what kinds of information are available. Iran and Tunisia rely largely on regulatory measures; Saudi Arabia and the UAE have, predictably, spent vast fortunes on technical solutions. No solution is foolproof, but the governments seem satisfied that their respective solutions ameliorate the dangers acceptably.

The rest of the MENA countries can be characterized as Driven: They want what the information revolution offers, and want it badly enough to be willing to risk some disbenefits that may arise from more open and possibly "unacceptable" communications. Those that have, get. The wealthy countries, including Bahrain, Kuwait, and Qatar, have well-developed information infrastructures. The poorest country, Yemen, has achieved very little. The middle-tier countries, Egypt, Jordan, Lebanon, Morocco, and Oman, have made interesting but unexceptional progress. Commercial relationships and personal influence are as important in these countries as is the availability of investment funds.

SOCIETY

The social implications of these developments are potentially wide-ranging. The information revolution is attempting to occur at a time when these countries are already suffering from rapid population growth, economic stagnation, and increasing demands for women to be more openly integrated into public life.

The potential for ICT to empower women through better education and less-constrained communications and to generate their own incomes should not be underestimated. Traditional mores are being challenged in all of these countries, and the Internet especially is making a large contribution. One Saudi prince opined several years ago (Goodman et al., 1998) that his wife's evening AOL (America Online) sessions made up to some extent for the restrictions on her ability to meet people—male and female—in person, but he failed to sense that this situation would not satisfy her for very long.

The governments and commercial sectors of the Driven countries understand that the information revolution can create jobs and revive local economies. The job markets have not kept pace at all with the increasing numbers of young people entering them; this situation has been exacerbated to the extent that women are now going to work, too. A new class of "information workers," likely to be largely female, may be emerging.

OUTLOOK

It is unlikely that any country in the Middle East or North Africa, including Turkey but possibly with the exception of Israel, will fully enjoy an information revolution during the next decade. There are too many impediments and too few champions, and—in most countries—too few resources.

Fewer than three people in 10 even has a telephone line, much less access to and interest in the Internet. Forecasts suggest that five in 10 people will have telephones by 2012, but other newly developed countries such as Korea and Singapore already have teledensities in excess of 100 percent.

The smaller, wealthier states have made the most progress toward information-centric futures, seeking to replace oil revenues that will diminish over time with other intangible products befitting their small sizes and lack of industrial base. The others will continue to muddle along, excepting Algeria and Iraq, which will have to solve domestic security issues before they can think much about the future.

AFP   Agence France-Presse

AHDI   Alternative Human Development Index

AHDR   *Arab Human Development Report*

AIS   *Armé Islamique du Salut* (Armed Islamic Front) (Algeria)

AOL   America Online

ART   Arab Radio and Television (Egypt)

BGP   Border Gateway Protocol

CAIDA   Cooperative Association for Internet Data Analysis

CDLR   Committee for Defense of Legitimate Rights (UK, anti-Saudi)

EIU   *Economist* Intelligence Unit

ESCWA   United Nations Economic and Social Commission for Western Asia

ESIS   European Survey on the Information Society

FBI   Federal Bureau of Investigation (U.S.)

FBIS   Foreign Broadcast Information Service (U.S.)

FIS	*Front Islamique du Salut* (Islamic Salvation Front) (Algeria)
GDP	Gross Domestic Product
GEM	Gender Empowerment Measure
GIA	*Group Islamique Armé* (Armed Islamic Group) (Algeria)
GPRS	Generalized Packet Radio System
HDI	Human Development Index
ICT	Information and communication technology
InfoDev	Information for Development Program
IR	Information revolution
IRNA	Islamic Republic [of Iran] News Agency
ISP	Internet Service Provider
ISU	Internet Service Unit (Saudi Arabia)
IT	Information technology
ITU	International Telecommunications Union
KACST	King Abdulaziz City for Science and Technology (Saudi Arabia)
MBC	Middle East Broadcasting Centre (UK)
MEM	Microelectronic machines
MEMS	Microelectronic Mechanical Systems
MENA	Middle East and North Africa
NGO	Non-Governmental Organization
NIC	National Intelligence Council
NIO	National Intelligence Officer

OECD	Organization for/of Economic Cooperation and Development
PC	Personal computer
SDNP	Sustainable Development Network Programme (UN)
telecom	Telecommunications company
U.S.	United States
UAE	United Arab Emirates
UAEnic	UAE Network Information Center (World Bank)
UK	United Kingdom
UN	United Nations
UNDP	UN Development Programme
UPI	United Press International
URL	Uniform Resource Locator
VOA	Voice of America
WTO	World Trade Organization

Chapter One

INTRODUCTION

The Middle East was once home to the world's most advanced societies, its people skilled at mathematics, astronomy, science, and medicine, and renowned for their poetry and arts. That epoch coincided roughly with the maximum extent of the Islamic empire, the remnants of which today are lumped together as "the Middle East and North Africa" (MENA), as listed in Table 1.1. The region is again becoming more closely integrated with the global economy, its people are traveling more widely and continuing to emigrate to the West

Table 1.1

The Countries of the Middle East and North Africa

The Middle East	
Levant	Arabian Peninsula
Israel	Bahrain
Jordan	Kuwait
Lebanon	Oman
Syria	Qatar
	Saudi Arabia
	United Arab Emirates
	Yemen
The Persian Gulf	
Iran, Iraq, and six Arabian Peninsula countries bordering the Gulf	
North Africa	
Maghreb	Mashriq
Algeria	Egypt
Morocco	Libya
Tunisia	

in record numbers, social unrest brought about in large part by poverty continues, and the spread of information and communication technology (ICT) continues to spur economic development. The ability and willingness of these countries to allow, encourage, and invest in their own information revolutions may have serious consequences for the foreign policy, affairs, and trade of the United States. This report summarizes the state of information and communication technology in the MENA region, with a view toward understanding the implications for the region's further economic development.

At least the technical elites of the countries of the MENA region have been aware of and discussing the imperatives of the information revolution for more than a decade. According to a Syrian academic, Dr. Sami Khiyami (1994), there was broad recognition even in the early 1990s of the dangers of being "left behind again," as the region had been following the Industrial Revolution. But recognition of the potential problem did not lead quickly to action. With the exception of (obviously non-Islamic) Israel, the countries of this region are what Hundley et al. (2001) refers to as "IR Conflicted Societies," populations that have been experiencing various levels of conflict between their traditional cultures and aspects of the new information society.

Most governments in the region had issues more important than the information revolution to tackle. For the richest governments, trade expansion and infrastructure investment were top priorities. Development of the ICT sector occurred principally as an adjunct to economic expansion, although the propensity for the elites of these countries to educate their children in the West provided a base of potential users of high technology who had both the skills and the expectations to spur ICT development. For the poorest governments, feeding the population, maintaining and occasionally improving the most basic elements of the infrastructure, and keeping the domestic peace consumed the governments' attention.

ICT development followed a typical Third World pattern: Deployment lagged behind need, and effective employment lagged behind deployment. No national policies were set for the development or use of information technology, although some efforts were made to improve and expand computer science education at the secondary-school and university levels (Burkhart, 1994). A pioneering role for the academic sector was typical of all MENA countries (Goodman et al., 1998), especially during the early days of the Internet.

While the proliferation of conventional voice telecommunications, i.e., the telephone, has been almost universally seen as having large benefits to society and few or no disbenefits, the development of the media—television, radio, and newspapers and other periodicals—has been controlled by regional governments. The arrival of the Internet has caused a great deal of concern. Governments and religious authorities were concerned lest the Internet be used "inappropriately";[1] academics were concerned lest they miss an opportunity to become more closely integrated with the major seats of learning and invention; and businessmen were concerned that they would at least miss out on the benefits of being wired to broader markets and possibly get left out of the "new economy" altogether. Security services were universally opposed even as the state-owned telecommunications companies viewed the Internet as a potentially bottomless well of new income. In Chapter Two, we briefly characterize the ICT infrastructure in the Middle East and North Africa, establishing the physical baseline, and take a look at technology.

Building on the research already conducted in this information-revolution project, we next explore the various dimensions of the MENA information revolution—economic and business, sociopolitical, political/governmental, and security—in Chapters Three through Six, using the set of causative and resultant factors that Hundley (n.d.) postulated to distinguish one nation's progress toward an information revolution from the others. *Causative factors* enable or retard the information revolution; *resultant factors* are the effects of the information revolution (IR) that can be used to characterize the nation's IR posture. Tables 1.2 and 1.3 recap Hundley's dimensions.

Continuing the analysis of the IR dimensions, we examine the economic and business dimensions for evidence of the spread of the "new economy," especially e-commerce, as well as the ways in which

---

[1]The definition of *inappropriate* has usually included anti-government and pornographic information. Countries with strong Islamic leadership, such as Saudi Arabia, also prohibit access to information denigrating Islam or extolling or proselytizing for other religions.

Table 1.2

Causative Factors Shaping a Nation's IR Posture

Technology Dimension	Social/Cultural Dimension	Political/ Governmental Dimension	Business/ Financial Dimension
Amount and quality of research in information science and technology	How the society deals with change	The nature of the legal regime	Degree of risk-taking mentality and entrepreneurship
	• Reaction to change	Degree and nature of governmental control	
	• Mechanisms for change		Structure of capital markets
		Degree of financial and institutional support for IT research	
Status of underlying physical infrastructure and human capital			

SOURCE: Hundley (n.d.).

Table 1.3

Resultant Factors Characterizing a Nation's IR Posture

Technology Dimension	Business/ Financial Dimension	Political/ Governmental Dimension	Social/ Cultural Dimension
Degree and nature of IT penetration into society	Amount of information work and number of information workers	Presence (and number) of new political actors (e.g., NGOs)	Degree of societal tension created because of IR developments
Distribution of IT activity across technology, artifact, and service spectrum	Amount and nature of e-commerce	Degree to which the role and manner of governance has changed	
	Presence (and number) of IT business clusters		
Amount of "creative destruction"			
Movement of talented, IT-trained people (into and out of country)			

SOURCE: Hundley (n.d.).

ICT is changing age-old work methods. Next to national security, this is one area that can be particularly affected by the uptake of technologies that make information, a critical source of power in these traditional societies, more widely and rapidly available and useful than before.

The social dimensions are equally important, given the economic roots of the antisocial phenomena that lure young people into terrorism. Is the "digital divide" closing or growing? The role of women in society is also being profoundly affected by modern communications, and e-learning is spreading literacy and, once again, information. Have these modern technologies altered in any fundamental way the social compact between the governors and the governed?

The next chapter takes a look at "e-government" and how some early initiatives have fared. The last dimension examined is security. The proliferation of modern ICT has spurred advances in both the maintenance of and opposition to domestic security.

We then take a deeper look at the differences between the ways the information revolution has affected the various subregions and countries, in Chapter Seven, and consider what countries might be "left behind" and what the implications might be for those that are, in Chapter Eight. If the digital divide continues to grow, what will be the impact of further marginalizing society's poorest members? Will some countries "miss" the revolution and be irrevocably left behind? Finally, in Chapter Nine, we review the dimensions and variations previously discussed for their policy implications for the United States. The diffusion of modern ICT will have profound affects on MENA countries. Opportunities will abound for the United States to influence and enhance this diffusion.

Chapter Two

INFORMATION INFRASTRUCTURE AND TECHNOLOGY

Every type of physical infrastructure, including, for example, surface and air transport and electrical power, is required for social and economic progress, including an information revolution. But the ICT infrastructures are the most directly relevant and often the only infrastructural elements that can be affected by ICT-related industries, organizations, and government agencies. The ICT physical infrastructure is made up of the fixed and mobile telephone networks, installed base of computing hardware and software, computer networks (some of which are carried, however, by a telephone network), and an international telecommunications bandwidth. The Internet and its associated international connectivity are the most relevant computer network and the core of the information revolution.

PHYSICAL INFRASTRUCTURE

In an earlier study in this series, Hundley (n.d.) classed the underlying physical infrastructure as a "causative factor in shaping a nation's information revolution posture." But the revolutionary process is cyclical, and today's infrastructure is the result of earlier ICT development efforts (which, in turn, were based on the then-existing infrastructure).

Telecommunications have been greatly improved throughout the MENA region over the past 10 years, but most countries remain well below world averages for number of telephone lines, international links, and, especially, Internet connectivity and services. Table 2.1 provides the International Telecommunication Union's (ITU's) 2001 compilation of basic ICT indicators. Although the Gross Domestic

Table 2.1

ICT Indicators (2001)

MENA Country	Telephones per 100 Inhabitants	Personal Computers (PCs) per 100 Inhabitants	Internet Users per 10,000 Inhabitants
Algeria	6.36	0.71	19.27
Bahrain	67.15	14.18	1,988.65
Egypt	14.63	1.55	92.95
Iran	18.70	6.97	62.29
Iraq	na	na	na
Israel	128.46	24.59	2,304.86
Jordan	27.12	3.28	409.11
Kuwait	48.79	13.19	1,014.71
Lebanon	40.74	5.62	858.00
Libya	11.83	na	35.84
Morocco	19.60	1.31	131.45
Oman	21.34	3.24	457.49
Palestine	16.82	na	181.21
Qatar	56.76	16.39	655.74
Saudi Arabia	25.81	6.27	134.40
Syria	12.09	1.63	36.12
Tunisia	14.90	2.37	412.37
United Arab Emirates	111.66	15.83	3,392.39
Yemen	3.01	0.19	8.89
United States	110.87	62.25	4,995.10
World Averages	32.77	8.42	823.24

NOTE: na = not available.

Product (GDP) per capita of Israel is less than half that of the United States, Israel has a higher telephone penetration rate. In contrast, Israel's information-technology penetration is roughly proportional to its relative GDP. The region's wealthiest country (per capita) is tiny Qatar, with only about 600,000 inhabitants, of which only about 150,000 are citizens. But the telephone penetration in Qatar is only half that of the United States, and the country is seriously lagging behind in computer ownership and Internet users. Yemen is the only country in the region classified as one of the world's "Least Developed Countries" by the United Nations and World Bank, and the paucity of ICT in the country reflects that status. In fact, the infrastructure in Yemen in general is so poorly developed and unreliable that the late editor of the *Yemen Times* speculated that the principal impediment to the spread of information technology was the lack of reliable electrical power (Goodman et al., 1998).

The United Arab Emirates (UAE) was not the first MENA country to connect to the Internet; even Iran was online earlier. But the perceived potential economic benefits were so great that the UAE government invested heavily in Internet infrastructure and service and continues to do so. The UAE Network Information Center (UAEnic) recently confirmed (Emirates, 2002) that the country had the highest Internet penetration of all the Arab countries, with more than 30 percent of households and almost half of all businesses online.

As in other underdeveloped countries, mobile telephones are not only a supplement for the well-to-do, but also a substitute for a land-line, the waiting list for which is many years long in all MENA countries. During the Lebanese civil war, for example, a privately owned mobile telephone network that routed calls through New York City was one of the only reliable communications channels in the country, particularly for international connections.

The proliferation of telephone service has been greatly enhanced by the continuing cost reductions in installing mobile (cellular) telephone lines. Thus, cellular service has been the main driver of teledensity increases in most countries, MENA countries included. But, thus far, this proliferation has had little effect on the diffusion or use of the Internet. New, broadband wireless technologies notwithstanding, computer networking is still accomplished mainly through the fixed telecommunications network. The explosion in wireless communications and predicted ubiquity of computers forecast in Anderson et al. (2000) has not reached the MENA region and is unlikely to have a major influence in most of those countries over the next ten years. Possible exceptions include Jordan and Egypt, which have in fact enjoyed explosive subscriber growth over the past two years. Azzam (2002) reports that mobile-telephone penetration varies from a high of 68 percent in the UAE to a mere 5.7 percent in Egypt, despite the rapid growth in the latter country. Only 12 percent of the residents of wealthy Saudi Arabia have mobile telephones, and the penetration is about 20 percent in both Lebanon, which has had competing private operators for many years, and Jordan, where mobile telephony has only recently taken off. Although Jordan's

MobilCom does offer mobile Internet access via 2.5G technology (Generalized Packet Radio System, GPRS), the service is not common in the MENA region. Upgrades to 3G technology, truly wideband mobile data networking, will lag well behind world averages.

Even in the poorest countries, the telephone companies are profitable. Over the next 10 years, both the fixed and mobile telephone networks in most MENA countries will continue to grow, based principally on reinvestment of profits. With the exception of Iran, which has developed a significant manufacturing capability, MENA networks will continue to be installed and often operated by foreign companies. Increasingly, today's favored Western vendors will be replaced by lower-cost suppliers from the Far East. Just as the Taiwanese PC manufacturer Acer has established a significant market presence based principally on pricing, other Asian ICT manufacturers will establish a bridgehead. The mainland Chinese have been especially aggressive over the past five years and have made some headway in the poorer countries. The Chinese government has learned from the West to offer subsidized financing tied to local vendors and is expected to continue a multi-market push into the region, selling everything from diapers (nappies) to cordless phones to surface-to-surface missiles, ostensibly as a lower cost and politically neutral alternative to Western suppliers.

TECHNOLOGY INFRASTRUCTURE

There continues to be relatively little independent research and development in the MENA countries.[1] Wealthy countries have no incentive; poor countries have no ability. However, in the middle ground, some impressive developments have taken place, albeit spurred by foreign investment, training, and know-how.

Residual hard feelings following Napoleon's withdrawal almost two hundred years ago notwithstanding, a strong link endures between Egypt and France, and the French have a long history of investment in Egyptian infrastructure and manufacturing. Today, the French are investing in such high-tech industries as microelectronic machines

---

[1]For example, "There is no R&D culture in Dubai," says the UAE's Abdel Qader Kamili (2002).

(MEM) and telecommunications (Bernard, 2002). Such investment benefits both parties: Egypt gains new industries, facilities, and trained staff—an updated industrial infrastructure; the French gain cheap labor. There is an increasing awareness that the growth in the number of Western-educated cadres and the improving education in some MENA countries are producing a ready source of highly educated, if poorly experienced, labor. Add experience and *voilá*: an annual personnel savings of more than 90 percent. Alcatel, the French telecommunications giant, has translated its investment in Egypt into a regional hub serving 28 countries. The open question is whether and how local elites and/or governments will translate these gains into long-term, systemic development.

Technical education, especially computer literacy, has received increased attention in the past 10 years and has improved, albeit slowly and unevenly. Almost all of the countries, with the probable exception of Libya, have established computer science and related curricula, beginning in the elementary schools. In the wealthiest countries, computer literacy has been supported by an extensive deployment of PCs throughout the educational system. At the higher grade levels and the universities, Internet connections are common. Although the local universities continue to grow, a degree from a Western higher-learning institution is still a coveted prize. On the Arabian Peninsula, American universities are favored, followed by British schools. In most of North Africa and the Levant, a French education is the first choice. An increasing number of students head for Canada and Australia, which are viewed as "good values," with fewer bureaucratic impediments.

A salutary development was the implementation in late 2000 of an Arabic-character-set URL (Uniform Resource Locator) system under the auspices of the Arabic Internet Consortium in Dubai, UAE. This development was said by Simon (2001) to ensure the growth of the "Arabic Internet" to more than 30 million users by 2005. (Today, Arabic and Farsi combined make up less than 1 percent of Internet language use, whereas Dutch accounts for 2 percent and Korean almost 4 percent.)

The intentions, but not the capabilities, have been mirrored in the less-wealthy countries, many of which are still not able to provide a basic education for every child. In Syria, for instance, a computer-literacy implementation developed by a national society with the education ministries has been hampered by the inability of the government to buy more than a few thousand PCs each year and by the lack of qualified teachers. The result is continued uneven development in the region and another obvious widening of the gap between the haves and have-nots.

ICT PENETRATION

Touring the region's capitals, it is easy to get the impression that PCs are ubiquitous. A closer look, however, reveals that, while almost every vendor's stall has a computer, the computers are generally decades old and are used for simple accounting and stock management. They have not changed the way business is conducted, but have only replaced manual tools. Telephones are everywhere, too, especially cheap Asian cordless phones, and almost every country has a reasonably robust cellular network in its capital city. But far more people can be seen walking around with a cell phone plugged into their ears in the UAE than in Damascus or even Beirut, where having at least one cell phone is considered *de rigueur*.

Once off the beaten path, computers and telephones disappear, and it is easy to get the completely opposite impression. And the beaten path is much narrower in the poorer nations than in the Gulf. The most widespread ICT presence is television, spurred by the proliferation of Ku-band satellite television channels, which can be received by small and relatively inexpensive—even in the poorest countries—antennas. Every government in the region has established at least one national satellite television channel, in part to spread its message throughout its own population, but also to compete with neighboring countries. As the number and variety of Arabic-language television channels have increased, so too has the production quality—because of the competition. The result is that a larger portion of the viewing population today prefers regional television to Western programming than it did 10 years ago (Maurice, 2002; Mulhem, 2002). While the West's attention has been focused on Al-Jazeera, people in the region have been tuning in Egypt's Nilesat and Dubai has been beaming its satellite programming to Diaspora audiences in Europe and South America. Thus far, the proliferation of satellite television has been made possible by government investments, including seed funding for Al-Jazeera, which runs out this year. To the extent that they are government organs relying on government funding, the further expansion of these networks will depend upon their marginal utility to the government. Moves have been made to privatize a couple of the networks, but governments are reluctant to give up their total control of programming, and alternative funding is uncertain. Subscription services have limited audiences, especially in the poorer countries, and the advertising markets in the region are not well developed.

ALTERNATIVE FUTURES

The wealthiest countries in the region will continue to expand their already-substantial networks and offer a greater variety of value-added services in order to continue to increase their profitability. Unconstrained by finances, the ultimate shapes and uses of these networks will depend almost entirely upon the governments' continued efforts to control information access. In countries such as Bahrain, Kuwait, Qatar, and the UAE, government will likely limit its control to pornography and other illegal activity (e.g., fraud, gambling). Besides wealth, these countries have in common reasonably stable and secure governments.

The big exception is Saudi Arabia, where the long-established social contract will continue to be renegotiated with an increasingly restive polity. The House of Ibn Sa'ud is in little danger of being overthrown. However, the combination of relative economic hardship (i.e., because of the reduction or elimination of personal subsidies due to lower oil earnings), increased exposure to foreign (not just Western) cultures, and an increasingly cosmopolitan, Western-educated and information technology (IT)-savvy middle class will put pressure on the government's paternalism. In both Saudi Arabia and Iran, the religious elites supported by, supporting, and controlling these governments will be forced to choose between their particularly austere visions of Islamic piety and peaceful streets. The choice will be all the more important as the economies come under increasing pressure to gainfully employ and offer a future to their growing youth populations. Economic development also will rely increasingly on being able to participate in the Information Age.

The middle-tier countries, Egypt, Jordan, Lebanon, Syria, and Tunisia, for example, will continue to expand their physical infrastructures, and ICT penetration will continue without any fundamental changes in the societies. The priority in all these countries will be to maintain the peace according to local interpretations of the social contract. The governments of Tunisia and Lebanon, for example, will be fully occupied with economic-development initiatives while the ruling parties attempt to maintain control. Egypt will continue to appear at once as a police state and a burgeoning free-for-all. Whereas the Saudi and Iraqi governments tightly control information dissemination and alternative voices, Egypt and Lebanon will continue to host a cacophony, which the governments rely on in part to disguise their control and to share any blame.

Syria will be an interesting country to watch, with its urgent need for economic growth and international acceptance sought, but curtailed, by the ruling minority and its supporters. Little by little, the government has shown an inclination to join the Information Age, but it is feeling its way cautiously—too cautiously say some leading businessmen, who already feel the future slipping away from them.

Oman is interesting just because it is so boring. The slow, well-considered growth that it has enjoyed over the past 30 years will continue in this country, where even the souks are swept at night. Neighboring Yemen, on the other hand, will remain boring despite the pace and variety of activity because of the sheer magnitude of the need for every manifestation of modernity, starting with clean water and stable electrical power. It has been said that Yemen's national heritage can be described as "change without progress," whereas the Kingdom of Saudi Arabia's is "progress without change." The former could be said to be something of a steady state, but the latter cannot continue forever.

Chapter Three

ECONOMIC AND BUSINESS DIMENSIONS

The causative factors in MENA countries are not favorable to the information revolution. The societies are generally risk-averse and conservative. Business decisions take time. And while it seems that everyone is "in business," Western-style entrepreneurship has been rare. Capital markets are nonexistent in some countries, such as Libya and Syria, and strongly state-dominated in most of the other countries. Even in countries with a well-developed private financial sector—countries that depend on that sector for a large portion of their earnings—the regulatory environment is strict. Thus, investment funds are very limited. The most significant source of development financing in most of these countries comes from international and regional lenders/grantors, such as the World Bank or Arab Bank for Regional Economic Development.

Similarly, there is relatively little investment in research and development in general, and almost none in information technology. Such efforts as exist seek principally to adapt a foreign technology to local conditions or develop an indigenous production capability, particularly for software development.

A notable exception is the investment being made by the French firm MEMScAP to create an Egyptian subsidiary that will develop and manufacture microelectronic mechanical systems (MEMS) for the European market. The stated reason for locating its subsidiary in Egypt was the availability of highly educated, albeit inexperienced, engineers at one-fourth the cost of their Western counterparts (Bernard, 2002). The French telecommunications giant, Alcatel, is also expanding its operations in Egypt beyond installation and maintenance of fixed- and mobile-telephone networks. The company has set up a software development house and a training subsidiary for technicians from other African countries. Again, the economics of the ventures were the key interest, and the Egyptian government, recognizing the need for high-tech investment, has stayed out of the way.

By contrast, an attempt by the Information for Development Program (infoDev), a multilateral assistance program sponsored by the World Bank, to conduct a symposium and feasibility and requirements study for setting up a Cyber Park ICT business incubator in Morocco—e-MAROC—stumbled on the ultimate unwillingness of the Moroccan government to commit half of the modest funding required (infoDev, 2002). The e-MAROC effort was subsequently canceled.

The prospects for more entrepreneurial actors on the MENA business landscape are somewhat favorable, although it remains to be seen whether and how they can increase the rate of business creation or transformation.

THE HEAVY HAND OF THE STATE

Not only are the capital markets generally highly controlled, but the infrastructure in most MENA countries remains in the hands of the state, practically eliminating private capital as a source of development. The trend today is privatization, but it has been far more effective on paper than in fact. The issues for these countries include the incentives for entry into the World Trade Organization (WTO) and prospects for investment on the one hand, but the perceived loss of control on the other hand. Typical of its halfway measures, Saudi Arabia recently "privatized" the national telecommunications carrier, converting it into a private stock company, but one in which the government owns all of the stock. Public sales of shares in the company have been repeatedly delayed. Table 3.1 gives an overview of the privatization of the ICT infrastructure in Egypt, as assessed by a European study group (ESIS, 2001). The Egyptian case is representative of the general state of privatization throughout the region.

Table 3.1

Telecommunications Liberalization in Egypt, 2001

Services	Status
Infrastructures	
Public telecommunications network	State monopoly
Leased lines	State monopoly
Alternative infrastructure	Nonexistent
Data transmission	State monopoly
Subscriber (pay) television	State monopoly
Television broadcasting	State monopoly
Cable television	State monopoly
Voice Telephony	
Local communications	State monopoly
Domestic long distance	State monopoly
International communications	State monopoly
Provision of voice services to closed user groups	State monopoly
Pay telephones	Private operators
Value-added services	State monopoly
Mobile Communications	
Analog	Nonexistent
GMS digital	Two private operators
DCS 1800 digital	Nonexistent
Mobile data transmission	Private operators
Paging	State monopoly
Satellite communications	One private operator
Internet services provision	60 private operators

SOURCE: ESIS (2001).

THE BUSINESS OF MEDIA

That the private sector is getting involved at all in the media marks a sea change in the policies of most MENA governments. Privately owned newspapers and magazines are still unknown in some countries and are barely tolerated in others. All the more surprising, then, is the extent to which the private sector has been allowed to offer Internet services.

Computers and communications, the physical infrastructure of the information revolution, are two of the three pillars of IT. The third pillar is content. Anderson et al. (2000) postulated that content is used for command, control, and commerce, with the last including entertainment.

According to Mustafa (2002a), political constraints mean that most "private media ventures focus on business," and *media business* in the MENA region means entertainment. This focus has produced an increase in the number of television-production concerns, principally in the free media zones in Amman; Beirut; Cairo, Egypt; and Dubai. The quality and variety of locally produced programming have increased accordingly.

But the media breakthroughs remain the province of offshore satellite television broadcasters, such as London's Middle East Broadcasting Centre (MBC), owned by the wealthy Saudi Shaykh Al-Waleed bin Talal (also formerly the majority shareholder in United Press International [UPI] until its divestiture in 2000), the Cairo-based-but-Saudi-owned Arab Radio and Television (ART), or the Rome-based Orbit network. The only exception is Al-Jazeera, the much-written-about satellite station of the Qatari government, and the motives and modalities of Al-Jazeera's breakthroughs remain moot.

ICT TRADE IS BOOMING

The lack of investment notwithstanding, the regional market for ICT goods and services remains vibrant and continues to grow (Niewiaroski, 2002). This growth is fueled by vendors of Western high-technology goods and services. The downside, of course, is that this burgeoning sector will continue to put pressure on foreign-trade deficits in the countries less well endowed with oil wealth, given the paltry level of local research, development, and production, and does little to raise the overall contribution of the MENA region to global development.

Western (American) vendors, such as Microsoft, IBM, and US Robotics, report sales increases ranging from a mere 26 percent to nearly 200 percent for Internet infrastructure equipment. And personal computer sales continue to grow, although they are mostly a case of "them that has, get," with the poorest countries recording almost no gains in private PC ownership. The worldwide slowdown in the IT sector has not hit the MENA region, because the regional market is not anywhere near saturation and oil prices have profited from the post-9/11 supply jitters. The forecast is for continued growth over at least the next five years (Niewiaroski, 2002). While the current market is estimated to be about $4.6 billion, the Aberdeen Group believes that, by 2005, it will have grown to more than $34 billion, with roughly equal growth in the goods (hardware and software) and services components.

E-CONOMY

The *Economist* Intelligence Unit (EIU) annually assesses the e-readiness of the world's 60 largest markets, which include Algeria, Egypt, Iran, Israel, and Saudi Arabia. Of these five countries, only Israel is in the upper half of those markets and all five have achieved lower ratings this year than last year (Table 3.2). Three reasons cited by the EIU (2002) for the lower performance of the Arab countries were poor IT infrastructure, lack of financing, and business cultures not conducive to e-business.

One of the more important effects of the Internet on economic activity, the increased availability to producers of current pricing information (Booz Allen, 2002b), is being felt throughout the Gulf and Levant. Even in relatively backward Yemen, construction companies have reduced the cost of their input factors (raw materials) by as much as 30 percent through the smarter tendering and ordering accomplished using the Internet (Goodman et al., 1998). This effect

Table 3.2

MENA E-Readiness Rankings, 2002

Country	E-Readiness Ranking (of 60)	2001 Ranking	E-Readiness Score (of 10)[a]
Algeria	58 (_)	54	2.70
Egypt	48 (_)	40	3.76
Iran	53 (_)	50	3.20
Israel	26 (_)	23	6.79
Saudi Arabia	47 (_)	44	3.77

SOURCE: EIU (2002).

[a]The factors assessed by the EIU include connectivity and technology infrastructure, business environment, consumer and business adoption, social and cultural infrastructure, legal and policy environment, and supporting e-services.

has not been universally welcomed, of course: Local vendors used to captive markets have had to reduce their prices and improve services to remain competitive. As discussed elsewhere, transparency is a novelty threatening to many in societies used to carefully controlling the availability of information, however much the economy as a whole benefits.

The government of Italy is sponsoring an e-procurement Internet site for Jordan to provide online trading, auctions, and settlement of bills (AP, 2002b). This will be the first major attempt at online commerce beyond the wealthy UAE and perhaps a useful barometer of how well and quickly regional markets will embrace digital business portals. While such portals have proven over time to have limited utility in the West, they may be of greater importance in a region where business information is hard to come by and often unreliable.

To what extent e-commerce really can take hold in North Africa and the Levant, regions in which hard-currency earnings and foreign-trade reserves are critical to the day-to-day operations of the governments, remain to be seen. As Indonesia discovered to its chagrin several years ago, the near-instantaneous flow of money goes in both directions. How can e-commerce take hold in a country like Syria, where there is no private capital market and the government watches the flow of every dollar, or in Yemen, which, for all practical purposes, is bankrupt? The answer lies in the investment patterns of the elite, and they are unlikely to change in the near term.

While this may be adequate for the elites and major businesses, there is no clear migration path to indigenous online commerce. Tax evasion is a national pastime in most of these countries; governments seeking to increase tax revenues impose usurious rate schedules. The resulting tax revenues remain flat at best, because taxpayers attempt to shield income from the previous round of tax hikes. The result is a huge hard-currency overhang, with literally billions stashed in offshore accounts and business conducted by letters of credit based on these accounts and credit cards issued by Western banks and covered by these same overhanging funds.

Chapter Four

SOCIOPOLITICAL ISSUES

The information revolution is about much more than technology. It would no doubt be helpful if we could place a laptop in the hands of every man, woman, and child in the Arab region. But there would still be issues of cost, access to the Internet, and the freedom for men and women to communicate equally with the outside world. These social and economic issues must be addressed throughout the Middle East if we can expect to see ICT used to achieve broader social and economic goals, such as increased literacy and the eradication of poverty.

ARAB WOMEN AND THEIR ROLE IN THE INFORMATION REVOLUTION

It is interesting, if not heartening, to reflect upon the role women played in science and technology during the course of prehistory and history. Women were the first technologists. They developed tools and devised methods to gather food, plant crops, make clothing, and heal illnesses. Women made everyone's lives easier and more productive—for themselves, their families, their communities, and subsequent generations. Ease and production are what technology provides for us today.

If women were the first technologists, what has happened in the Middle East, a place we think of as the cradle of civilization? More than half of all Arab women cannot read or write.

Most Arab women today are mired in decades upon decades of cultural quicksand layered purposely by male-dominated societies that have squelched women's intellectual, innovative, and entrepreneurial abilities and denied them their rightful place in society. This historical gaffe is costing Arab nations dearly today.

"Sadly, the Arab world is largely depriving itself of the creativity and productivity of half its citizens," says the United Nations' first *Arab Human Development Report* (UNDP, 2002), released July 2, 2002, in Cairo. "How can a society compete in an increasingly globalized world if half of its people remain marginalized and disempowered?"

In an overall sense, women have made great strides in Arab countries over the decades, the *Arab Human Development Report* (AHDR; UNDP, 2002) reveals. The region shows the fastest improvement in female education of any region, with female literacy expanding threefold since 1870. And, of course, Arab nations vary with respect to women's rights and ICT accessibility.

But women have a long way to go in the Arab world (UNIFEM, 1995).

> It is not acceptable for women to constitute 70 percent of the world's 1.3 billion absolute poor. Nor is it acceptable for women to work two-thirds of the world's working hours, but earn only one-tenth of the world's income and own less than one-tenth of the world's property. Many fundamental changes must be made."
> —Noeleen Heyzer, Director of the United Nations Development Fund for Women.

Male-dominated Islamic cultures often lean on religious traditions as an excuse for the disempowerment of women. However, nothing could be further from the truth. The teachings of the Holy Prophet of Islam emphasize "the acquiring of knowledge as bounden duties of each Muslim from the cradle to the grave" and that "the quest for knowledge and science is obligatory upon every Muslim man and woman" (Hassan, 2000).

So there is no religious or cultural basis for the discrimination against women or the refusal to tear down the social and cultural barriers that deny the female half of the population access to higher education, technology, and political and economic participation.

"The [AHDR] report acknowledges progress made by Arab countries in some areas of development, notably in increasing life expectancy, at birth, and reducing infant mortality," Dr. Rima Khalaf Hunaidi, assistant secretary general and director of UNDP's Regional Bureau for Arab States, said in testimony before the U.S. Congress on August 24. "Moreover, there is much less dire poverty in Arab states than in any other developing region."

"But the report also flags some warning signs that cannot be ignored," Dr. Hunaidi testified:

> Growth over the past two decades has been the lowest in the world, except for Sub-Saharan Africa. Labor productivity has been on the decline since 1960. Sixty-five million people are illiterate. One out of every two women can neither write nor read. Ten million children are out of school. Unemployment has reached 15 percent, with regional hot spots suffering from much higher rates: 50 percent.

Three key deficits showed up as ADHR researchers traced the roots of the crisis:

- A freedom deficit is stifling creativity and true participation.

- A woman's empowerment deficit is depriving societies of half of their productive potential.

- A knowledge deficit is weighing heavily on the ability to grow and compete (Hunaidi, 2002).

In addition, ICT education is lacking, telecom reform is moving slowly, and Internet access is too expensive for many Arab families.

The Arab team at the UN Development Programme (UNDP) has come up with another measure: the Alternative Human Development Index (AHDI). This excludes rankings such as income per capita, but adds measurements to the HDI that take into account a country's record on freedom, use of the Internet, and carbon-dioxide emissions. Predictably, Arab countries do even worse when they are measured this way.

It is bad enough that all aspects of Arab society have been stifled by slow technological growth, but the ADHR reveals that the region's lagging participation in the information revolution is likely to result in a major brain drain: 51 percent of all adolescents and 45 percent of pre-teens expressed a desire to leave the region altogether—presumably for the Western world (Hunaidi, 2002).

One clue to viewing the problem realistically may lie in taking a frank look at the "Gender Empowerment Measure" (GEM), established in the UN's 1995 *Global Human Development Report.* The GEM ranking identifies participation of women as reflected by income per person, women's share of professional and technical positions, and women's share of parliamentary seats (UNDP, 2002).

The Arab region had an overall GEM ranking lower than almost anyplace in the world, running a close second to sub-Saharan Africa. Moreover, the GEM scale revealed that Arab countries as a whole had less participation by women in the workplace than anywhere else in the world. And, with only 3.5 percent of parliamentary seats filled by women, the Arab region weighed in with the world's lowest GEM score for political involvement.

Remedies in the Face of Gender Bias and Other Realities

The *Arab Human Development Report* concludes that the solution lies in adopting and implementing a three-pronged strategy that simultaneously addresses building human capabilities:

- Implementing quality education, health, and social services, and quality research and development activities, to promote creativity and technological empowerment.

- Using human capabilities through revitalizing the economies and providing equal opportunities to all, especially women.

- Liberating human capabilities through promoting systems of good governance. Good governance would include reforming state institutions and activating the voice of the people (Hunaidi, 2002).

As to ICT, "The region is trying to bridge the digital divide, but it will be a very gradual process," says Arab League Secretary-General Amr Moussa (LaMotte, 2002). And bridging that divide will require an enormous commitment on the part of governments, donors, and the private sector. If successful, such a plan could give people in Arab countries the tools as well as the hope for a better life. However, if goals are not met on time or as expected, the alienation, apathy, and discontent that often arise in such situations could be damaging. Therefore, plans for growth must be realistic. Any effort to bridge the gap needs to focus on (Hunaidi, 2002)

> Simultaneous measures for building, using and liberating human capabilities. Estrangement and frustration arise not only when one is deprived of capabilities such as quality health and education, but also when one is deprived of the opportunity to use such capabilities in productive employment due to economic stagnation or legal biases, or when such capabilities are stifled by lack of freedoms or through systems of government.

ICT as a Tool for Women's Economic Empowerment

Because the success of ICT-based economies rests heavily on the participation of the entire population, developing such economies to be open to women as well as to men not only provides new opportunities for women but also serves Arab countries in general.

The introduction of new technology into the Arab world provides the perfect vehicle for women to boost their social status in the community and raise their self-esteem by making a much-needed contribution to the workforce.

Although Internet penetration is exceedingly low in the Middle East, many Web sites are available in Arabic as well as in English to women in the Arab world. Some are even specifically designed for women, such as www.arabwomenconnect.org, which is sponsored by the United Nations Development Fund for Women.

But, of course, availability means nothing if the tools and access to the Internet are not present.

The United Nations had two meetings scheduled in 2002 to facilitate women's access to new technology:

> "Information and Communication Technologies and Their Impact on and Use as an Instrument for the Advancement and Empowerment of Women," in the Republic of Korea, 11–14 November 2002.

"Participation and Access of women to the Media and Its Impact on and Use as an Instrument for the Advancement and Empowerment of Women," at the United Nations Economic and Social Commission for Western Asia (ESCWA) in Beirut, Lebanon, 12–15 November 2002.

In preparation for the meetings, women were invited to join weekly chat sessions to voice their opinions on a broad range of topics related to women's empowerment and ICT (WomenWatch, 2002).

IT IS NOT JUST ABOUT THE INTERNET

All Arab countries need assistance in building ICT infrastructure and providing tailored technology solutions. *Tailored* is the key word. There is a tendency to look at the Internet as the global solution that can solve all needs. But providing development assistance to facilitate access to the Internet is often too much too soon:

In some cases, Internet use may prove too expensive or too difficult for local people to maintain, and thus be unsustainable. And in others, the Internet is simply not the best medium for supporting local socioeconomic and political progress (Alcántara, 2001).

Another impediment to Internet usage is that most content is still in English. More efforts to create content in Arabic will undoubtedly raise the level of Internet use in Arab countries.

Cynthia Hewitt de Alcántara (2001) addresses the differences among Third World countries in their capacity to use information technologies for development:

The ICT revolution is lending old technologies new relevance. In many parts of the world, mobile telephones are transforming people's quality of life. New digital radio stations are reaching a wide public in an interactive way through call-in programmes.

Furthermore, in the process of designing an appropriate local strategy for using ICT to the benefit of disadvantaged groups, success will depend at least as much on understanding the structure of economic and political constraints affecting people's livelihood as on remedying immediate problems of access to ICT, says Hewitt de Alcántara.

ISLAM ON THE INTERNET

Islamic texts and discourse venues have been available on the Internet for about 20 years. Anderson (2001) discerns three phases to the growth of an Islamic presence on the Internet: "technological adepts," people who uploaded scanned texts and added a generally laic discourse; "activists and official voices," individuals at two ends of the ideological spectrum, competing for adherents; and "spokespersons and audiences," people representing the "online advent of moderate Islam." Throughout this maturation process, Anderson notes that the principal actors in each phase used and even furthered the development of the best publicly available technology.

The United Nations Economic and Social Commission for Western Asia (ESCWA, 2002a) has taken a look at several Arab countries. The reports on Jordan and Qatar are of particular relevance.

Jordan

The most recent census, conducted in 1994, indicated that illiteracy rates for adults in Jordan were 9.9 percent for men and 20.6 percent for women. At 10.7 percentage points, the gender gap is significant. However, for those who were enrolled in formal education, the gender gap was minimal in lower grades and practically zero in secondary schools. Moreover, the textbooks used in Jordan's schools portrayed women in highly derogatory terms, ESCWA reports.

Jordan has invested steadily in information and communications technology. The ICT sector is believed to offer better opportunities for enhancing the role of women in the economy than traditional work offers, because as a relatively new sector, gender is less of a problem than elsewhere.

A 2001 study conducted by the National Information Centre in Jordan revealed that the rate of participation of women in ICT at a managerial level was 13 percent for the private sector and 30 percent for the public sector. Women programmers account for 22 percent of all programmers in the private sector and 50 percent of all programmers in the public sector.

Several initiatives have been put forward to narrow the digital divide and to promote "e-quality" in ICT. In July 2001, UNIFEM and Cisco Systems Inc. launched a US$2-million joint project entitled "Achieving E-Quality in the Information Technology Sector in Jordan." The project intends to establish gender academies with Cisco networking certification and to enable female students to build upon their current technological knowledge with demand-driven networking skills to increase their competitiveness in the labor market.

In October 2001, a workshop entitled "Women in ICT: Reaching for Success" was held in Amman. The gathering of highly influential women in the one-day event hosted by the Information Technology Association in Jordan showcased efforts on behalf of women in the country's IT sector.

Furthermore, the Internet is seen as a powerful tool for raising gender awareness. In 1998, SIGI established a pilot training and technology-based node in Amman in which facilities are available to representatives of Non-Governmental Organizations (NGOs) working on issues pertaining to women. In November 2000, UNIFEM launched an innovative Web site to empower women: http://www.arabwomenconnect.org.

Qatar

The Internet service provider is the satellite-based telecommunications company (telecom) Q-Tel, started by the government of Qatar and now partially privatized. Of Q-Tel's 10,000 subscribers, 30 percent are women. Some 60 percent of those women are thought to be nationals, and it is believed that they are largely decisionmakers.

Qatar is a haven for Arab males who seek a more Western culture. In 2000, non-nationals made up 73.7 percent of the total population in Qatar. And since immigrants there tend to be men in the 25–49 age group, women represented only 35.4 percent of the total population—a disproportionately high ratio of men to women in Qatar.

In 1999, the illiteracy rate was 17 percent for women and 20 percent for men. Women marry later and have a lower birth rate. Life expectancy is 77 years for women and 73 years for men, well above the world average of 67 years.

Women in Qatar enjoy freedom and opportunities unheard of in most Arab nations. At the University of Qatar, 72 percent of students are women. And in technology, women represent 59 percent of the student population.

There is no question that Qatar is one of the leading nations in the Arab region in access to the Internet. Experts attribute this fact to a relatively free press and an open-door policy toward ICT. The existence of satellite broadcasting has had a major influence, as well.

For women in a male-dominated society, the Internet provides a window onto the world in Qatar. It is thought that women use e-mail and Internet services more than do men because their command of English is generally better. Since the rise of the Internet in 1996, 30 percent more female nationals started taking classes to improve their English-language skills.

Q-Tel, the telecom of which more than half is government owned, leases lines to 11 girls' schools and nine boys' schools. Of the 10 Internet cafes in Doha, three are for the exclusive use of women.

A technology information center has been set up in the Ministry of Foreign Affairs and includes a women's unit, in which some female nationals work.

ACCELERATING TECHNOLOGICAL CHANGE

The current rapid pace of technological change is expected to accelerate over the next 15 years. In addition to increasing the digital divide between the world's richest countries and those that even today cannot keep pace with change, rapidly changing technology and its associated industries will place a premium on education and training. Education and training are already front-burner issues for every government in the region. According to Antón et al. (2000),

> Cultural adaptation, economic necessity, social demands, and resource availabilities will affect the scope and pace of technological adoption in each industry and society over the next 15 years. The pace and scope of such change could in turn have profound effects on the economy, society, and politics of most countries.

This cannot be good news for MENA countries, which have shown a proclivity for resisting any form of cultural adaptation. Furthermore, variations in the degree of economic necessity (e.g., between the richest and the poorest, a divide that is already great), social demands (which are increasing everywhere, but more alarmingly in the most conservative countries), and resource availability will tend to continue the increase in wealth, health, and modernity in general throughout the region.

Chapter Five

GOVERNMENTS AND THEIR OPPONENTS

Governments throughout the Middle East and North Africa attempt to exercise strong centralized control over commerce, finance, and politics. Many extend their control into the social sphere and people's private lives. None of these governments came to power as a result of what the United States would term a free and fair election. This situation at once reinforces the need for centralized control to retain power while fomenting opposition, and, when coupled with the dire economic straits of many of these countries, greatly enhances the potential for violence. This has spawned and supported such general opposition to central government as the *Ikhwan al-Muslimeen* ("Islamic Brotherhood"), which at one time or another has been opposed to almost every Arab government; local opposition groups, such as the Islamic Salvation Front (*Front Islamique du Salut*, FIS) in Algeria; or some of the mountain tribes in Yemen. Even in countries that have held what were the fairest elections in their histories, such as Iran and Lebanon, a significant portion of the population feels disenfranchised.

Where the social compact between the government and the governed is bankrupt, information and communications technologies become powerful weapons for both sides, but are of limited use to voices of moderation.

KNOWLEDGE IS POWER

A central fact of both commerce and governance in MENA countries is that the powerful have established and maintain their power to a great extent by controlling the dissemination of information. The

Iraqi government to this day has not told its people that their army was crushed by the coalition forces in 1991, and attempts to prevent that information from entering the country through various forms of censorship. Businessmen jealously guard information of every sort about their operations and the market. Seniors hide data from juniors and dole it out only to the degree absolutely necessary or to bestow a favor. The power of ICT to disseminate data more widely and efficiently and to create transparency in government and business operations is inimical to most of the ruling elites.

The regional governments figured out long ago the power of the media to deceive, and many have attempted to harness the power of modern technology, especially the Internet, to increase their control over the populace: "New media in all its channels can be used to disseminate old material and content" (Abu Hijleh, 2002). They have discovered that it is possible to create at least an image of transparency by providing information outlets that appear to answer questions and enlighten while stifling unwelcome inquiries. Such outlets include automated dial-up information and fax-back services, call-in television appearances by government and religious officials, and, especially, government Internet sites. The propensity has thus been to attempt to reap the benefits of the information revolution while avoiding giving up control.

THE "DICTATOR'S DILEMMA"

On the one hand, the information revolution cannot occur in the absence of a reasonably free society, although freedom is not the only prerequisite. On the other hand, implementation of ICT tools for government and commerce introduces the dangers posed by greater access to information, including increasing desires for personal and commercial freedom and improved standards of living. Table 5.1 compares subjective ratings of freedom and the information revolution in the MENA region.

What emerges from the table is the suggestion that a real information revolution will have little chance of occurring in any of these countries except Israel. The corollary is that all the other governments have reasons to be concerned lest the encroaching technologies engender aspirations for greater political freedom and civil liberty. The situation described by then–Secretary of State George Schultz almost

Table 5.1

Freedom and the Information Revolution

Country	Political Rights	Civil Liberties	Freedom Rating	How Info-"Revolutionary"
Algeria	6	5	Not Free	Not At All
Bahrain	7	6	Not Free	Moderately
Egypt	6	5	Not Free	Trying
Iran	6	6	Not Free	Cautious
Iraq	7	7	Not Free	Not At All
Israel	1	2	Free	Very
Jordan	4	4	Partially Free	Trying
Kuwait	4	5	Partially Free	Moderately
Lebanon	6	5	Not Free	Moderately
Libya	7	7	Not Free	Not At All
Morocco	5	4	Partially Free	Trying
Oman	6	6	Not Free	Intending
Qatar	6	6	Not Free	Moderately
Saudi Arabia	7	7	Not Free	Very Cautious
Syria	7	7	Not Free	Desirous
Tunisia	6	5	Not Free	Trying
United Arab Emirates	6	5	Not Free	Trying
Yemen	5	6	Not Free	Not At All

NOTE: Source for Political Rights, Civil Liberties and overall Freedom Ratings: Freedom House (2002). The higher the numerical score, the less free the attribute. For a detailed explanation of the scores, see http://www.freedomhouse.org/research/freeworld/2000/methodology5.htm.

two decades ago and subsequently styled the "Dictator's Dilemma" (Kedzie, 1997) is still relevant:

> Totalitarian societies face a dilemma: either they try to stifle these [information and communication] technologies and thereby fall further behind in the new industrial revolution, or else they permit these technologies and see their totalitarian control inevitably eroded. In fact, they do not have a choice, because they will never be able entirely to block the tide of technological advance.

But today's tide is not merely one of technological advance, it is accompanied by political, social, and personal aspirations riding in on the tide of wider and richer communications.

In the countries that have invested heavily in ICT, is the adoption of modern information technology driving political change? Have new, IT-enabled actors appeared on the scene? There does not appear to be a single instance of a change in the political landscape because of the spread of information technology. Indeed, there has been little political change of any type in this region in two decades. The same combination of strong central control and conservatism that stifles change has prevented any expansion of the political environment or major actors. While the Internet in principle provides NGOs with greater access to the MENA population, there is no evidence that this has had any impact, for two reasons. First, the Internet is principally an "information pull" network: No information is provided that is not sought. While e-mail can be, and is, used by dissident and other organizations outside of the region (e.g., Christian religious organizations, gay rights groups) to inject alternative views into society, e-mail is easily ignored or blocked. Second, the Worldwide Web itself is strictly a pull network. And, again, the regional governments can and do block a wide assortment of Web sites. Those who work to circumvent this blockade are already activists whose political or religious views were formed independent of any information revolution, although some of their activities may be facilitated by Internet links.

Two innovations that do stand out are the extensive use of the Internet by contenders for elective office in Iran and the use of a nationwide network by the ruling party in Yemen to dynamically manage elections (Goodman et al., 1998). In neither case, however, has the range of political actors or the depth of political discourse been increased; the Internet has simply been used as an additional communications channel.

How has the proliferation of ICT changed governance in the region? Is the Internet-fed quest for ever more information creating any demand for transparency? The only effect thus far has been to allow some governments in the region to become more efficient without fundamentally altering the nature of their governance. Such changes as have occurred, notably the establishment of *Shura* ("people's") Councils in several Gulf states, had their genesis in the early 1990s, before the Internet made any significant inroads in the region.

We found no evidence that the pace or nature of political change has been affected at all by any nascent information revolution, although Hudson (2001) proposes that "the evidence is scant," believing that the combination of globalization, driven in part by IT, and the coming of age of a new generation of leaders will engender the development of a "new Arabism" that will facilitate the redistribution of power and influence. He goes on to suggest that this new racial consciousness will be created in large part by the proliferation of news and information sources, including and especially satellite television broadcasting in Arabic, which makes these alternative views accessible to the common person (bearing in mind the scarcity of computers and high rates of illiteracy).

Therein lies the seed of what Hudson expects to be significant "creative destruction" as the new Arab polity finds its voice. Ultimately, according to Hudson's logic, the states will be unable to keep the information genie in the bottle that has been at least cracked open by the new media.

In our judgment, it will come down to determining whether maintaining the status quo is worth significant repression of new thinking and voices—the path followed in Iraq—or whether power in the modern age is best exercised through economic forces. We have already seen evidence of the latter, particularly in Syria, a relatively freewheeling police state whose masters are busily exchanging guns for hard currency. This does not mean that significant economic liberalization has occurred, only that the masters are using more subtle tools.

THE SOCIAL CONTRACT

The relationships between the governing and the governed—the *social contracts*—in MENA countries is under stress. Only three of these countries, Iran, Israel, and Lebanon, have reasonably democratically elected governments, but even those are under pressure. However, there is no evidence that any aspects of an information revolution have caused or are even contributing significantly to the pressure. The principal causes of challenges to the social contracts arise from a perceived lack of real pluralism in such countries as Iran and Lebanon, from significant economic changes in such countries as Saudi Arabia, and from other social causes, such as increasingly youthful populations whose ranks are growing faster than the economies can employ them and such repressive regimes as in Algeria, Iraq, and Libya.

PROGRESS WITHOUT CHANGE—E-GOVERN-NOT

The tiny state of Qatar, an innovator in a number of spheres, was the first Arab government to go online, having initiated an e-government pilot project in early 2000 (BBC, 2000a). This project followed early success in the public-works sector, which made online "kiosks" available to the public for obtaining utility work permits and retrieving records. Goodman et al. (1998) reported that, by 1998, all government agencies were online and had access to common databases. The entire country had been rendered digitally, and projects were under way to map public utilities and other infrastructure. Making these data available to contractors and city planners online and via kiosks was a logical and successful next step. The 2000 pilot project, which was to have been completed by late 2002, would provide for electronic processing of all forms and reports, both between government agencies and offices and with the general public. With an Internet penetration of less than 10 percent (see Table 2.1), the deployment of public-access kiosks is the only way to connect electronically with the population.

One of the aims of the e-government pilot was to eliminate the long waiting lines in the various ministries. Whether e-government can significantly reduce those lines or simply move them out of the government's offices onto the sidewalk remains to be seen. And, of course, the prospect for any change in the underlying governance is negligible.

Another example of an e-government initiative that really does not alter the political landscape is ongoing in Tunisia. The same Italian program that is to set up e-commerce services in Jordan (see Chapter Three) is outfitting the Tunisian government's tax collectors with electronic databases to improve their performance and, presumably, increase the government's revenue collection (AP, 2002b).

In Jordan, even the *Mukhabarat* ("secret police") is online (http://www.gid.gov.jo/) in a show of openness that is not backed up by the content or services offered. Note, however, the awareness of intellectual property demonstrated by the up-to-date copyright notice.

In Qatar and the UAE, the leaders have decreed that the ministries and departments will participate in the Internet, so these governments are well represented online. The principal effect has been to make some of their operations more efficient through speedier communications and sharing of databases, but there still is no suggestion of any e-government initiatives like those unfolding in the West. The e-government initiative of Dubai, for instance, has as its goal "to facilitate the dealings of the public and the business community with the government" by making it as simple as possible to wend one's way—electronically now—through the bureaucracy (Obeidat, 2002). The guiding principle in Dubai is that time is money. Because time saved is money earned, speeding up the bureaucratic processes will have a real economic impact. Equally important is the provision for people and businesses to pay their fees online, i.e., without having to trudge to some ministry or department, thereby, it is hoped, increasing revenues and speeding their collection.

Meanwhile, Saudi Arabia announced that it "tops Middle East nations" in its readiness for e-government (ITP, 2002a). How is it so ready? In mid-2002, the government was "preparing to choose" a vendor for the first phase of its e-government system, which will produce the Saudi Gateway for intragovernmental communications and the Saudi Public Data Site as a gateway for exporting data by the government "to the Internet."

ENEMIES AT THE (VIRTUAL) GATES

MENA governments are beginning to address a new media phenomenon: the virtual proximity that the Internet affords offshore dissident groups and the Diaspora communities in general. The most interesting example is offered by Iraq, which has almost no domestic presence on the Internet.

According to Fattah (2002), essentially no Iraqi presence on the Web originates from within Iraq, and the offshore Web presence can be divided into opposition groups espousing the overthrow of Saddam Hussein and groups seeking an end to international sanctions on Iraq. (It should be noted that these two groups comprise many more constituents than the Iraqi Diaspora.) Fattah goes on to say that the Internet has given "Iraqi cyber communities a stake in the country's future, and allowed them to debate questions they were unaccustomed to raise back home." But who is the audience and what is the potential effect of such debate? For Iraq, it is doubtful that the ongoing Web dialogs have any impact whatsoever in Iraq, if indeed they are even noticed. The proximal targets of the lobbying are the United Nations and Western governments, but the real audience is most likely other expatriate Iraqis—a community talking to itself.

The same cannot be said for some of the most vocal opposition to the Saudi government, although the ultimate impact is probably just as low. By far the most vocal and prolific opponent of the ruling Saudi monarchy is the Committee for Defense of Legitimate Rights (CDLR), a London-based group that has been "broadcasting" its anti-regime message into the Kingdom via facsimile ("fax-blasting") for decades. However, the addition of the Internet, both Web and e-mail, to its arsenal has done little to increase its reach into the Kingdom. Arguably, while Internet communications complement CDLR's other activities, they reach a smaller audience in Saudi Arabia than do CDLR's more traditional communications.

ENEMIES (NOT) ONLINE

As poorly as the governments may be doing, they are still light-years ahead of the opposition in most cases. Table 5.2 suggests an "electronic correlation of forces," comparing the "e-ratings" of the governments with those of their opposition. Just as the September 11th hijackers were unsophisticated but highly successful, so too is most of the opposition in the MENA region. With the exception of Jordan, Qatar, and the UAE, there is significant and often violent opposition to every government in the region. With few exceptions, however, the opposition has not taken to the Information Age, and none is more technically savvy or well-wired than the government.

Table 5.2

Electronic Correlation of Forces

Country	E-Government Rating[a]	Opposition "Loyal" or Otherwise	E-Opposition Rating[b]
Algeria	None	AIS	None
		FIS	None
		GIA	None
Bahrain	Moderate	Misc. Islamists	None
Egypt	Moderate	Islamic group	None
		Misc. opposition	Low
Iran	Low	"Hardliners"	Low
Iraq	None	Everyone	None[c]
Israel	High	Hamas	Low
		Hizbollah	Low
		Misc. Palestinians/groups	None
Jordan	Low	None significant	na
Kuwait	Moderate	Misc. politicos	Low
Lebanon	Low	Opposition parties	Low
		Syrian intelligence	Very Low
Libya	Very Low	Everyone	None
Morocco	Low	West Saharans	None
Oman	Low	Misc. Islamists	None
Qatar	High	None significant	na
Saudi Arabia	Moderate	CDLR (external)	High
		Misc. Islamists	Low
		Osama bin Laden	Low
Syria	Very Low	Muslim brotherhood	None
		Non-Alawite activists	Low
Tunisia	Low	Opposition parties	Low
UAE	High	None significant	na
Yemen	Very Low	Misc. tribes	None
		Unreconstructed Communists	None

[a]A factor of the degree of automation and networking internal to the government and externally with the populace.

[b]A factor of the degree of automation and networking internally and on the Internet.

[c]Various opposition groups in exile have a limited external Internet presence that is transparent to residents of Iraq. There is limited Internet connectivity between some Kurdish-controlled areas and the outside world, mostly for coordination with and fund-raising by supporters in exile.

Chapter Six

SECURITY CHALLENGES

"Security" as understood and practiced by MENA governments is much more all-encompassing than in the West. Several hundred years of authoritarian—or stronger—governments overlay the traditions of tribal societies, leading to a conservative polity that often appears less inclined to question government control than seems reasonable to Western observers. MENA governments' notion of a civil society envisions fewer freedoms than are taken for granted in the United States. Al-Khatib (2002) describes a government with such broad powers as "paternal."

This characterization is changing as globalization brings to the region images and ideas of greater personal freedom and responsibility, especially with the proliferation of television. Television eliminates the literacy barrier and addresses those sectors of society, such as women and the very poor, who have been the least exposed to alternatives to traditional mores. Globalization also provides the potential for the Diaspora to have a greater impact, ideologically and financially, than it has had in the past. While the governments continue to be ruled by the "traditional" generations, the increasing demands for a renegotiation of the social contract will continue the past decade's trend of increasingly vocal and violent opposition.

National security is intended to control and/or combat "anything that is a threat to the ruling institutions and their interests" (Goodman et al., 1998). These ruling interests include not only the senior government leaders, but also the Islamic religious authorities and leading commercial houses. The broader the definition of *security* is, the broader is the range of threats to be defended against, providing justification for levels of social control unacceptable in the West and increasingly questioned in the MENA region (Abu Hijleh, 2002):

> New media, whether satellite television channels or Internet, has contributed to the opening of passageways for fresh information and analyses that are free of the clout of subordination to governmental inclinations.

CENSORSHIP

Censorship of all media is expected and generally accepted, if not exactly welcomed. Addressing a forum on "New Media and Change in the Arab World" in early 2002, Fuad Abu Hijleh said, "It goes without saying that censorship of the media exists in all its forms in Jordan. . . ." He divided censorship not only into governmental and religious, which Western observers consider the norm, but also into "societal, . . . direct, indirect, institutional and auto-censorship," suggesting a much more pervasive intrusion into private life than one might expect.[1] Bear in mind, too, that Abu Hijleh is talking about one of the most ideologically progressive countries in the region. Michael Knights (2001) states that "the Gulf States have always recognized the unrestricted cross-border flow of information as a potential security threat."

Radio and television are identified by Abu Hijleh and others as the most important media institutions,[2] because they reach into every level of society and every corner of the country. The Internet gets most of the attention from students of globalization, but it is the unwritten word that remains of most concern to MENA governments.

---

[1]According to Abu Hijleh, *societal censorship* is the result of an inherently conservative society, while *institutional censorship* reflects the risk aversion of any bureaucracy. These are in addition to the explicit effects of overt governmental and religious censorship. *Direct censorship* is overt; *indirect censorship* is inherent in implicit disincentives, such as the fear of job loss. *Auto-censorship* is the result of the combined actions of all the others, and is in the end the most insidious.

[2]See, for instance, Al-Khatib (2002), who identifies television as "the most favored media to Palestinians." He further points out that, while more than three-quarters of Palestinians consider television their principal provider of information, fewer than one-quarter rely on Palestinian television, favoring other Arab satellite channels and even Israeli television over the local fare.

Note that the Jordanian government, which tightly reins in the press, radio, and television, has made no attempt whatsoever to control access to the Internet or any online content.[3] However, most governments are not so sanguine about the implications of the Internet. As Knights (2001) points out, the Gulf states "have been quick to react to the even greater threat to political stability, religious stricture and economic control that the Internet is believed to present."

See No Evil

Saudi Arabia provides the most extreme example of censorship, both in the pervasiveness of attempted control and in emphasis on the Internet as the main threat. The Saudi government has implemented a technically complex and expensive system designed to prevent Saudi Internet users from being able to access or view online content deemed inappropriate by the government.

e-Censorship. The government of Saudi Arabia established an interministerial commission that took no less than two years to study the Internet, document its pros and cons, and recommend means for reaping the benefit of the former while eliminating the latter (Goodman et al., 1998). Thus was born the Internet Service Unit (ISU) at the King Abdulaziz City for Science and Technology (KACST). The ISU is the sole point of inference between the Saudi telecommunications network and the Internet. It has established a highly complex network of redundant routers and firewalls intended to be unbreachable—not by hackers or other criminals, but by Saudi users wanting to see something banned by the government. Smart-Filter software from California's Secure Computing completes the system, although its contract expired earlier this year (Lee, 2001).

One section of the ISU comprises the censors, whose sole purpose is to find and block "inappropriate" material. Besides searching out such material on their own, they, like the censors in the UAE, accept anonymous recommendations from watchful citizens, who are said to contribute 500 new sites per day (Lee, 2001). Reports vary on just

---

[3]Very early in its Internet history, in the early 1990s, the Jordanian telecommunications ministry attempted to employ an e-mail filtering system to screen for legally or socially prohibited communications, but the system proved at once cumbersome and ineffective, leading the ministry to discontinue its use.

how much material is blocked. A recent Harvard Law School study, conducted with the knowledge and assistance of the ISU, found that more than 2,000 Web sites have been blocked (Hermida, 2002). Most of the blocked sites contain sexually explicit material or non-Islamic religious material. A partial listing can be found in Harvard (2002). The survey also found that the Saudis appeared to be attempting to keep Western pop culture out of the Kingdom, as well as information about health and medicine and women's issues, and bathing-suit catalogs.

An equally unrealistic figure was reported by Agence France-Presse (AFP) earlier in 2002, in a story that claimed that 200,000 new URLs were being added to the 400,000 already being blocked. While the Kingdom is almost certainly blocking more than 2,000 sites, attempting to keep track of more than half a million sites would seem unreasonably daunting. Even if no attempt was made to eliminate invalid URLs, the technical challenge of providing efficient access via a system that has such a large table to check would seem insurmountable. According to the AFP report, the ISU was adding 20,000 sites per month to its proxy servers.

e-Hajj. This year, the Saudi Ministry of Hajj ("the Pilgrimage") used the Internet, for the first time, to "improve the enjoyment and spiritual of the experience [sic] for tens of thousands of pilgrims." What spirituality does YaHajj.com provide? A government database of visa information, for one thing (ITP, 2002b). Although the principal and legitimate purpose of the system is to assist the Saudi hosts with logistics—lodgings and travel bookings, for example—security is another strong objective of the system. There have been no reports of how well the system worked or exactly what it was used for during the first Hajj for which it was employed.

When Is the "Free Zone" Un-Free?

Dubai is the most economically dynamic and arguably the most liberal of the seven emirates of the UAE. The Dubai Media City was set up in early 2000 for the "promotion of Dubai as a center for technology, e-commerce and media . . . to make Dubai a hub for the new economy" (Kamili, 2002). One of the basic strategies behind this free zone was to create an "environment and attitude" that would attract the world's leading companies. But an attitude toward freedom of expression that prohibits pornography (as defined by the local government), preaching about any religion other than Islam, and publication by political parties or related companies, and that bans "defamatory content," the definition of which is not very specific, may not be conducive to attracting the world's best.

OUTLOOK

There will be no relaxing of "security" as long as the governments remain imposed—whether by tribal custom and heredity, religious elites, or powerful minority coalitions—rather than popularly selected. The outlook for an information revolution, therefore, remains firmly tied to the outlook for political reform, which is bleak everywhere.

Chapter Seven

VARIATIONS IN THE INFORMATION REVOLUTION ACROSS THE MIDDLE EAST AND NORTH AFRICA

There is no single model for an information revolution. And, just as MENA countries are starting from different baseline conditions, the IR will play out differently in each country and the near- and midterm end states will vary widely. Differentiation among countries of the region is expected to grow, however, as some countries respond more effectively to the challenges of the information revolution and of globalization more generally. The effectiveness of their responses will be limited by the availability of investment funds and the conservatism of ruling elites.

The direction of global trends appears to bode for a poor IR in most MENA countries, whose conservative, change-resistant regimes and strong central governments have been thus far able to ignore and/or repress any forces for liberalization (NIC, 2000). The degree to which information revolutions occur in the region will depend in large part on the continued stability and attendant policies of today's ruling regimes. In analyzing a recent UNDP report on development in the Arab states, Symon (2002) characterized the governments' attitudes toward civil society as ranging from "opposition to manipulation to 'freedom under surveillance.'" She further noted that "while personal computers are more widespread in the Arab region than in any other part of the developing world outside Latin America, the region has by far the lowest Internet access and usage."

CENTRALITY OF THE INTERNET—AND MONEY

Simon (2001) characterized Internet development in the MENA region as falling into three categories: countries that allowed the Internet to develop essentially freely for the economic benefits it would bring, countries so fearful of potential adverse consequences that they banned the Internet, and countries that tried to have it both ways by fostering "acceptable" activity while tightly controlling the rest (similar to China's attempt at economic liberalization while maintaining tight political control). We agree generally with Simon's characterizations; however, we differ in our judgment as to which country belongs in which category. Our interpretation of the governments' policies and actions over the past 10 years are captured in Table 7.1 to be used as the starting point to extrapolate likely development courses over the ensuing 10 years.

Table 7.1

Wealth and Disposition Versus Development

Disposition Type	Country	Wealth	Internet Development
Driven	Bahrain	High	Rapid, extensive
	Egypt	Moderate	Moderate
	Israel	High	Rapid, extensive
	Jordan	Moderate	Slow
	Kuwait	Very high	Rapid
	Lebanon	Growing	Rapid
	Morocco	Moderate	Moderate
	Oman	Moderate	Slow
	Qatar	High	Rapid
	Yemen	Low	Very Slow
Fearful	Algeria	Low	Halted
	Iraq	Low	None
	Libya	Low-moderate	Recent, slow
	Syria	Moderate	Recent, slow
"Best of Both"	Iran	Moderate	Very slow
	Saudi Arabia	Very high	Recent, moderate
	Tunisia	Moderate	Moderate
	UAE	Very high	Rapid

Driven

Countries as different as Bahrain, Lebanon, and Yemen were all driven by economic imperatives. Most of these "Driven" countries are also the most liberal (or least illiberal), although even staid Kuwait put aside fears of Western culture, religion, and pornography in favor of reaping economic benefits. Interestingly, in both Kuwait and Qatar, early government efforts to spur Internet development concentrated on the educational sector, although the public sector was not far behind.

Among these Driven countries, the greatest differentiator with respect to Internet development is the nation's wealth. Wealthy countries did more, and faster, although they did not always have early starts. Poor Yemen brings up the rear again, although senior government officials and leading businessmen and academics have shown intense interest. But there simply was not enough money to do very much at all, and what was done was done primarily by foreign operators under contracts that resulted in Internet service charges that could be borne only by very few Yemenis. However, the open market for online services (although not international connectivity) did spawn interesting and, we believe, unique hybrids that attempted to provide a modicum of service at a modest charge.

The future for the Driven countries promises more of the same, with each country investing as much as it can and growing as rapidly as possible in order to achieve the full benefits of globalization. The main limiting factor will be money, but in many countries the Internet has proliferated widely enough to begin providing economic benefits significantly greater than the required investment. Private-sector investment will be the main source of capital, although public-sector financing will remain important in Jordan, which has a weaker economy than the others, and in Kuwait, for supporting the educational sector. Lebanon is likely to achieve significant growth haltingly, as the government's attempts to control information flows and the media wax and wane. Also, the Lebanese economy's significant and lasting downturn may also adversely affect private investment. The infrastructures in Bahrain and Qatar will fully meet demand within the next five years, although the degree of Internet use will depend on the pricing policies of the public sector–dominated Internet-service providers.

"Best of Both"

Continued success and growth in the "Best of Both" countries will depend upon the continued strength of the regimes with respect to popular pressures. These pressures are growing, and will certainly continue to grow over the next decade, in Iran and Saudi Arabia. The Iranian government's "schizophrenic" attempts to grow but control the Internet reflect the government's larger divisions between the "moderates" or "reformers" and the "hardliners." Iran's security and religious watchdogs clearly seek tighter controls and more-limited access, the educational and private sectors are attempting to achieve the opposite, and the public at large, that segment of the populace that has the education and means potentially to use the Internet, is generally in favor of unrestricted access.

Although the Saudi government has declared ICT development to "be a centerpiece of national policy" (Kashkoul, 2002), access to the Internet remains strictly controlled by the state, which maintains the only international gateway. This gateway is heavily guarded by multiple, redundant firewalls in what must be the most complex and expensive attempt at content filtering in the world. At the same time, the requirement to connect to a single, government-owned gateway using the government-owned telecommunications network allows the Saudi government to keep Internet access costs quite high relative to the income of the average citizen.

Internal pressures in Tunisia are unlikely to grow significantly, and the prospects for business as usual are good. The regime's policy toward the Internet will generally reflect the degree of tension between the government and citizenry at any given time. The government of the UAE has thus far been able to blunt public criticism by continued investment aimed at keeping network growth in line with demand. As long as they can do what they want for the most part and the service is relatively rapid, the general public does not seem to mind censorship too much. And then, those that do mind seem adept at finding ways around the censorship.

Fearful

The possible futures of the "Fearful" countries are quite varied. It is not possible to predict reliably how they might play out. It is possible, however, to describe the limiting factors and the probable outcomes of any changes in those factors.

In Algeria, it is possible that the level of domestic violence and the regime's repressive responses will diminish over time. If they do, the economy will start to grow again, albeit slowly. Algeria caught the first wave of the information revolution, but further development was quickly curtailed by the government in the face of domestic terrorism and open insurrection. Economic stagnation and the lack of pluralism fed extremist responses, which were answered in kind by the regime, generating an economic downturn and tighter government controls.

In Iraq, the prospects for any development, let alone an information revolution, are bleak. If the regime of Saddam Hussein remains in power or is succeeded by his supporters, no information revolution will occur. Saddam's control of the media and other information sources has been nearly as absolute as Kim Chong-Il's grip on North Korea, allowing the government to propagate its own version of recent history and current events. Only parts of the northern Kurdish regions have less restricted access to the outside world than the rest of Iraq, but these areas have other problems that will also preclude any progress toward an information revolution. Should Saddam be ousted and replaced by someone outside his clan, the future remains very uncertain. Since the Gulf War, the central government's control of the Kurdish regions and of the Shi'ite "Marsh Arabs" in the south has varied significantly and it is not clear how closely or how quickly any new Baghdad government could reintegrate these regions into a unified central government. Add to this situation the veritable elimination of the information infrastructure in Iraq and between Iraq and the outside world and it is clear that the possibility of widespread changes there over the next decade is less than remote.

Libya, on the other hand, appears to be emerging, however slowly, from its exile from the world community. Initially self-imposed, its exile was reinforced by international sanctions in response to Libya's support for terrorism. Despite the sanctions, Libya purchased and commissioned its first digital cellular telephone network in the mid-1990s. However, its attempt to commercialize that company failed, as did a faltering attempt to privatize the state telecommunications monopoly. Although Libya has oil income, that income is not well distributed and the bulk has been spent on a massive water-distribution project spanning more than a decade. It is possible that the Al-Qadhafi regime will continue to carefully loosen restrictions on commerce and connectivity in an effort to boost foreign-trade and hard-currency earnings. Although there have been several minor insurrections in recent years, the government faces no organized resistance and appears to understand that the best path to continued domestic peace lies in economic development, which, in turn, relies on trade and foreign investment.

Syria is also emerging from self-imposed isolation, although its continued occupation of Lebanon and the lack of a regional peace settlement will continue to hinder foreign investment and cause the government security headaches. The "informationization" of Syrian society has been championed by the new president and spearheaded by the Syrian Computer Society, two senior members of which were recently appointed to ministerial positions. The government is not as concerned about restricting access to particular sources of information or entertainment as it is about limiting and monitoring the communications resources potentially available to the regime's many enemies. Modern surveillance technology has done as much to spur the proliferation of communications media, especially the Internet, as has any other factor.

All in all, it is unlikely that a complete information revolution will occur in any MENA country, although many of these countries will benefit from the continued proliferation of information services.

Chapter Eight

WILL SOME COUNTRIES MISS THE INFORMATION REVOLUTION?

It is unlikely that any country in the Middle East or North Africa, with the possible exception of Israel, will fully enjoy an information revolution: There are simply too many impediments and the impediments are rooted in the conservative cultures, even when the resources—investment funds, technical know-how, etc.—are reasonably available. The only other country that might experience an information revolution is Lebanon. Its culture is more open and cosmopolitan than elsewhere in the MENA region, and commercial competition is keen. But the liberalization of Lebanon awaits the liberation of Lebanon from Syrian occupation and war with Israel.

Today, LaMotte (2002) estimates that a mere 1 percent of the region's population (excluding Israel) uses the Internet. These countries got late starts in joining the rapid global expansion of ICT deployment, and all but five continue to lag behind, well below average world-development indicators. Extrapolating current population growth and ICT proliferation rates suggests that no more than a few percent of the region's population will be using the Internet during the coming decade.

Less than 30 percent of the region's population (again excluding Israel) has a telephone line, compared with a world average of about one-third and teledensities in excess of 100 percent in Israel and such newly industrialized countries as Korea, Singapore, and Taiwan. It is likely that the region as a whole will deploy telephone service for at least half of the population by 2012, but there will be wide variations between the richest and most liberal countries on the one hand and the poorest and most repressive on the other hand.

The countries that will have made the most progress toward an information-centric future are Bahrain, Israel, Kuwait, Qatar, and the UAE. Note that these countries are "post-industrial," having skipped directly from an agricultural or nomadic base. With a foundation of oil, the Arab countries rely heavily on the financial sector and international trade as their sources of wealth. All are seeking to reduce their dependency upon oil, thus hastening the expansion of non-extractive, non-industrial activities. Israel could be well on its way to an information revolution, but will be hampered by the large and growing number of Arab citizens who represent a significant underclass that is unlikely to make much progress in the near term.

Will any country be left hopelessly behind? Most likely, Algeria and Iraq, both of which will likely suffer significant internal strife and leadership uncertainty for years to come, will be. Even when (if) the situation normalizes, it will take Iraq years just to restore pre-invasion conditions. ICT is not on the critical path to stability in either of these countries. Libya is likely to remain isolated and increasingly beset with internal strife. Knowledge is not power in Libya; raw physical power *is*. Yemen, absent reform, stability, and economic development, could continue to be a breeding ground for terrorists and a thorn in the region's side. Of potential interest, Yemen's strategic location at the confluence of the Arabian Peninsula, the Indian Ocean, and sub-Saharan Africa makes it a melting pot for peoples of different races, albeit mostly Muslims, and gives it the potential to control a strategic choke point. What does it matter that the Suez Canal is kept open if/when the southern end of the Red Sea is endangered? The Soviets understood this, but lost their grip. Will Yemen continue to try to work with the West to achieve at least a survival level of infrastructure development, or will it decide to exercise its strategic position to hold the West hostage? Note that, after France, the most prominent source of foreign aid to Yemen is China, which we noted elsewhere is giving the region the hard sell on its goods and services.

Then there is the gray area: countries that continue to increase the use of information technology without really achieving anything revolutionary. Chief among these is Egypt, for which continued development is critical for economic expansion, which is in turn critical for regional peace. All of Egypt's disaffected cannot be arrested and will not stay at home forever.

Syria has the potential to continue to be a spoiler in regional politics, fueling and hiding from international crises. Its large and aggressively commercial trading class urgently seeks any and all tools to further their interests, but it is in the end a country of traders and small manufacturers (carpets, sugar, pasta) rather than "information workers." ("Information workers" in the Middle Eastern sense conjures up visions of the secret police.)

Jordan, Morocco, and Tunisia will probably continue modernizing their infrastructures and perhaps enjoy some economic resurgence, but are unlikely to achieve anything revolutionary. None of these countries contributes significantly to regional politics or economy.

Oman, too, is likely to remain a backwater. It could be a major player in regional geopolitics if it could figure out what to do with its position opposite Iran in the Strait of Hormuz. Informationization is not on their critical path, however.

Lebanon will continue to be characterized by fractious local politics and aggressive international trading. Once the "Riviera of the Eastern Mediterranean" and a global banking hub, it is struggling to regain its stature of three decades past, but success is unlikely. Tourism is indeed picking up, but remains down overall throughout the region. The Gulf states have effectively taken over for good Lebanon's former role in international finance.

Chapter Nine

POLICY IMPLICATIONS FOR THE UNITED STATES

The Information Age is not dawning in the Middle East or North Africa, but significant changes will occur. Some of the changes will be affected by the proliferation of information technology, and some of the changes will affect the future of ICT development in the region. The information revolution is not a zero-sum game: All countries, cultures, religions, and peoples can ultimately benefit. But the very core values of the information revolution—freedom of expression, reciprocity between individuals, and universality of access (Franco, 1995)—are at odds with the implicit and seldom-stated national goals of every MENA country except Israel.

Whether information revolutions will take hold or fail relies to a great extent on the nature of the future regimes, which adds to the case for continued U.S. support of the development of democratic bodies and policies in this region. The United States has lost significant credibility over the past 10 years, however, because it has consistently supported such undemocratic regimes as those of Saudi Arabia, in the name of continued oil supplies; and Algeria, lest Islamists, however elected, take over the government. And the Israeli-Palestinian conflict continues to polarize many in the region, fueling anti-American sentiment.

As the U.S. government learned early in Operation Enduring Freedom in Afghanistan, this country needs to develop better capabilities for fighting the "battle of the airwaves"—the struggle for the minds and hearts of the public worldwide. This "battle" in turn requires better knowledge of the histories, cultures, and politics of these countries and significantly improved foreign-language skills. The generally low availability of Americans with foreign-language skills, especially in the high-interest but "low density" languages of the developing world, makes intelligence and other information collection and interpretation slower and more difficult, and significantly hampers the U.S. government's ability to make its own message heard.

And the airwaves on which the United States needs to do battle carry television programming, not radio. U.S. International Broadcasting's establishment of the *Sawa* Arabic service is sadly inadequate, and this inadequacy is compounded by the discontinuation of Arabic language broadcasting by the Voice of America (VOA). The medium of choice worldwide is television, which communicates ideas far more graphically than does radio, and the United States needs to be on television. The expensive and extensive reactions to foreign satellite television broadcasting by MENA countries are proportional to the effects the regimes expect this programming to have on their internal politics. To the extent that the United States wants— needs—to have a peaceful influence on regional politics, it needs to be on television. And television broadcasting also provides a cost-effective means of reaching more people with a more powerful message than is possible with radio. Satellite-distributed radio is in its infancy and unlikely to have a sizable audience in the near future, if ever (note that Radio *Sawa* is also relayed by Nilesat, Arabsat, and Eutelsat satellites). Terrestrial radio broadcasts have limited range, and attempting to reach widespread audiences, even on the long-range shortwave bands that used to be popular outside of North America, requires expensive infrastructure.

Today, Radio *Sawa* can be heard on the FM band only on the western littoral of the Persian Gulf; on medium wave in Egypt, the Levant, and the Persian Gulf region; and on shortwave three times daily. But television programming can reach every MENA country from one or two satellites and a single earth station. Although *Sawa* features Western and Arab music, it has been characterized by some regional journalists as a mouthpiece for the Central Intelligence Agency, since *Sawa's* director has said in the course of several interviews that its news programming is prepared and approved in Washington (Joha, 2002). An earlier Reuters report (2002) did not help when it said that Radio *Sawa* was associated with the White House's new Office of Global Communications. Note also that, although Iran continues to be of high interest to the U.S. government, Radio *Sawa* is not broadcast in Persian, and VOA's Persian Service is being gutted to divert funds for Radio *Sawa.*

Perhaps the single most important point about Radio *Sawa* is that it is also broadcast via the Internet and is hosted on a very appealing site in Arabic. However, the site carries neither transcripts of the radio broadcasts nor any other news. Therefore, an Arabic-language site with news and features from an American perspective could be highly valuable, especially if it were not run by the U.S. government.

To this end, it may be worthwhile to support, financially if necessary, the establishment of Arabic-language versions of major American newspapers' Web sites. *The Wall Street Journal* or *San Jose Mercury News* in Arabic could be quite compelling. Once the IT gap is bridged, the next hurdle in cyberspace is language. More generally, the U.S. government would be well-served by increased native-language content on the Web, not just Arabic.

POLICY CONUNDRUM OR OPPORTUNITY? AL-QAEDA ONLINE

Although not directly related to MENA governments, the use of new media by Al-Qaeda and other MENA-originated multinational terrorist groups is of increasing concern. The concern is not only about the proselytizing the organizations attempt via the Internet, but also about reports of the use of ostensible information sites as covert communications means. At bottom, however, we have almost no understanding of what media Al-Qaeda is using to communicate internationally. It is this lack of knowledge that appears to raise the most concern.

According to the Islamic Republic [of Iran] News Agency (IRNA) (2002), an Al-Qaeda Web site was hosted in Malaysia from January through May 2002. In May 2002, the Malay government shut it down and turned over the Web content to the U.S. Federal Bureau of Investigation. The Web site's contents were subsequently moved to a server in Texas and then to Michigan. Recent manifestations of the Al-Qaeda site have included al-neda.com, drasat.com (closed in late June 2002), and mnafe.com. Each of the sites was identical in form and content to the others. The Al-Qaeda site was reported to have disappeared from the Internet entirely in late July 2002. It is unlikely that the Al-Qaeda presence is no longer on the Internet.

What has Al-Qaeda and/or its supporters trying to accomplish, apparently going to great lengths to maintain a visible presence on the Internet? It has been suggested that the content contained coded messages, but none has thus far been discovered. The site was certainly intended to spread information of use to the entire "Al-Qaeda community," and possibly to direct cells and operatives to more secure communications means. But the ultimate intent may be the most obvious: to spread the gospel according to Osama bin Laden. He has made rather clever use of the other new medium prevalent in the MENA countries—satellite television—and the Internet provides an inexpensive adjunct, especially to the extent that it can be used to generate dialog with potential new supporters and recruits.

The other troubling aspect of the Al-Qaeda Web presence, beyond the question of its intended use and effectiveness, is that law enforcement officials in the several nations involved have been completely unable to identify the sources of the content or the funding for the Web sites. Payment for the Malaysian site was effected via Venezuela, under a false name and address. For the Texan site, the bill remained unpaid, which was the reason for Al-Qaeda being taken off that server, necessitating its move to Michigan.

Thus far, community protests and financial irresponsibility have made it difficult for Al-Qaeda to maintain a Web presence. But it has done so nevertheless. The move to the United States was especially interesting: Malaysia offers no First Amendment protection to the media. Al-Qaeda has been designated a terrorist organization by the U.S. government, but it remains to be seen whether and how it will be able to keep Osama bin Laden off the air. Does it even want to? Depriving Al-Qaeda of an Internet outlet will force it into other communications channels. Will those channels be easier to monitor? Is the site an effective means of proselytizing and recruitment? Which aspect is the most important? From a public diplomacy point of view, the U.S. government would seem to be obligated to exercise whatever means were at its disposal to deny Osama bin Laden a public forum. From an intelligence point of view, it might make the most sense to exercise enough pressure on the Web content's owners to keep them moving around, thereby creating a money trail or other link to the origin and ensuring that, to the extent that Al-Qaeda uses the Web site to communicate at all, the U.S. government can continue to observe and, it is hoped, come to understand those communications.

(Abu Hijleh, 2002) Abu Hijleh, Fuad, *New Media and Change in Jordan*, paper presented at the New Media and Change in the Arab World conference, Amman, Jordan, 28 February 2002, http://www.media-arabia.org/userfiles/Jordan%20Country%20%20English.doc (20 August 2002).

(AFP, 2001) Agence France-Presse, "Saudi to block 200,000 new Internet sites," *Al Bawaba*, 29 April 2001, http://www.albawaba.com/headlines/TheNews.php3?action=story&sid=158263&lang=e&dir=business (27 June 2001).

(Alcántara, 2001)   de Alcántara, Cynthia Hewitt, *The Development Divide in a Digital Age*, United Nations Research Institute for Social Development, 1 August 2001, http://www.unrisd.org/unrisd/website/document.nsf/ (httpPapersForProgrammeArea)/19B0B342A4F1CF5B80256B5E0036D99F?Open Document (26 August 2002).

(Al-Hassan, 2001) Al-Hassan, Mohamed J., "Born dead: The Internet in Saudi Arabia," *Al Bawaba*, 21 May 2001, http://www.albawaba.com/headlines/TheNews.php3?action=story&sid=161821&lang=e&dir=business (27 June 2001).

(Al-Khatib, 2002) Al-Khatib, Nabil, *Palestinian Media and the Effects of New Arab Media on the Information Process in Palestine*, paper presented at the New Media and Change in the Arab World conference, Amman, Jordan, 27 February 2002, http://www.media-arabia.org/userfiles/ACF8A8C.doc (20 August 2002).

(Anderson, 2001) Anderson, Jon W., *Muslim Networks, Muslim Selves in Cyberspace: Islam in the Post-Modern Public Square*, prepared for a panel on Public and Private Spheres in Muslim Societies Today: Gender and New Media, Conference of the Japan Islamic Area Studies Project on "The Dynamism of Muslim Societies," Tokyo, Japan, October 5–8, 2001, http://nmit.georgetown.edu/papers/jwanderson2.htm (15 October 2001).

(Anderson et al., 2000) Anderson, Robert H., Philip S. Antón, Steven C. Bankes, Tora K. Bikson, Jonathan Caulkins, Peter J. Denning, James A. Dewar, Richard O. Hundley, and C. Richard Neu, *The Global Course of the Information Revolution—Technology Trends: Proceedings of an Inernational Conference*, Santa Monica, Calif.: RAND, CF-157-NIC, 2000.

(Antón et al., 2000) Antón, Philip S., Richard Silberglitt, and James Schneider, *The Global Technology Revolution: Bio/Nano/Materials Trends and Their Synergies with Information Technology by 2015*, Santa Monica, Calif.: RAND, MR-1307-NIC, 2000, http://www.cia.gov/nic/graphics/rand.pdf (14 July 2002).

(AP, 2002a) "Looking for cheap software? Head to Gulf," Associated Press (AP), 3 August 2002, http://timesofindia.indiatimes.com/articleshow.asp? art_id=17961285 (4 August 2002a).

(AP, 2002b) "Italy sponsors technology transfer to developing countries," Associated Press, 8 August 2002, http://www.bayarea.com/mld/mercurynews/3822533.htm (8 August 2002b).

(Azzam, 2002) Azzam, Henry T., "Good prospects for mobile telephony in the Arab region," *Jordan Times*, 21 July 2002, http://www.menafn.com/qn_local_detail.asp?news_id=954 (24 July 2002).

(BBC, 2000a) "Qatar aims for online government," BBC Online, 13 March 2000, http://news.bbc.co.uk/1/hi/world/middle_east/675962.stm (4 August 2002a).

(BBC, 2000b) "Internet clampdown in Mecca," BBC Online, 17 April 2000, http://news.bbc.co.uk/1/hi/world/middle_east/716424.stm (4 August 2002b).

(Bernard, 2002) Bernard, Dan, "Partners in Tech?" *Business Today Egypt*, July 2002, http://www.businesstodayegypt.com/show_article.asp? a=0207CP_France&ch=Industry&p=BT (3 August 2002).

(Booz Allen, 2000a) Booz Allen Hamilton, *E-Commerce at the Grass Roots: Implications of a "Wired" Citizenry in Developing Nations*, Falls Church, Va., 30 June 2000, http://www.cia.gov/nic/graphics/grass_roots.pdf (14 July 2002a).

(Booz Allen, 2000b) Booz Allen Hamilton, *Foreign Legal and Regulatory Landscape: Its Effect Upon the Development and Growth of E-Commerce*, Falls Church, Va., 14 July 2000, http://www.cia.gov/nic/graphics/legal_landscape.pdf (14 July 2002b).

(Burkhart, 1994) Burkhart, Grey, *Information Technology in Syria*, September 1994.

(CAIDA, 2001) Cooperative Association for Internet Data Analysis, *BGP Geopolitical Analysis*, 27 November 2001, http://www.caida.org/analysis/geopolitical/bgp2country (14 July 2002).

(Economist, 2002) "Self-doomed to failure: Arab development," *The Economist*, 6 July 2002, http://www.economist.com/displayStory.cfm? Story_ID=S%27%29H%24%2DP%217%2A%21%20%214%0A (24 August 2002).

(EIU, 2002) *The Economist Intelligence Unit E-Readiness Rankings, July 2002, The Economist*, 12 July 2002, http://www.ebusinessforum.com/ index.asp?layout=rich_story&doc_id=5768 (31 July 2002).

(El-Ganady, 2002) El-Ganady, Mansour, "Accounting for culture," *Business Today Egypt,* June 2002, http://www.businesstodayegypt.com/show_article. asp?a=0206SO_maxgains&ch=Finance&p=BT (3 August 2002).

(Emirates, 2002) "UAE marches towards networked society," *Emirates Bulletin*, No. 161, July 20, 2002.

(ESCWA, 2002a) United Nations Commission for Economic and Social Development in Western Asia, *Country Profile: Qatar*, Social Development Issues and Policies, Women and Development,

2002, http://www.escwa.org.lb/divisions/social/profile/jordan/main.html (20 August 2002a).

(ESCWA, 2002b) United Nations Commission for Economic and Social Development in Western Asia, *Country Profile: Qatar*, Social Development Issues and Policies, Women and Development, 2002, http://www.escwa.org.lb/divisions/social/profile/qatar/main.html (20 August 2002b).

(ESIS, 2001) *European Survey on the Information Society (ESIS) Master Report: Regulatory Developments in Egypt*, January 2001, http://www.eu-esis.org/script/notice.cgi?fic=EGreg7.htm&repertoire=esis2reg&search_for=egypt&domaine_p=on&domaine_a=on&domaine_o=on&domaine_r=on&zone=EG&=&=&appel=simple (25 July 2002).

(Fattah, 2002) Fattah, Hala, *The Iraqi Diaspora on the Net: Rooted or Rootless?* paper presented at the New Media and Change in the Arab World conference, Amman, Jordan, 27 February 2002, http://www.media-arabia.org/userfiles/Hala%20Fattah%201st%20paper.doc (20 August 2002).

(Franco, 1995) Franco, Gaston Lionel, ed., "A wholly new world: Visions of the unfolding era (III)," *World Communications*, "Le Monde Economique" series, October 1995.

(Freedom House, 2002) "Freedom in the world 1999–2000," *Freedom House*, 17 July 2002, http://www.freedomhouse.org/ratings/index.htm (13 August 2002).

(Gardner, 2000) Gardner, Frank, "Qatar aims for online government," BBC Online, 13 March 2000, http://news.bbc.co.uk/1/hi/world/middle_east/ 675962.stm (4 August 2002).

(Gentzoglanis et al., 2001) Gentzoglanis, Anastassios, Nancy Sundberg, and Susan Schorr, *Effective Regulation Study: Morocco 2001*, International Telecommunications Union, 2001, http://www.itu.int/itudoc/itu-d/publicat/ma_ca_st.html (28 July 2002).

(GIIC, 2002) Global Information Infrastructure Commission 2002 Annual Forum, *Forum Report*, April 21–23, 2002, Beijing, PRC, http://www.giic.org/annualfor/China_Annual_Forum.PDF (27 July 2002).

(Goodman et al., 1998) Goodman, Seymour E., Grey E. Burkhart, William A. Foster, Laurence I. Press, Zixiang (Alex) Tan, and Jonathan Woodard, *The Global Diffusion of the Internet Project: An Initial Inductive Study*, March 1998.

(Hannoun, 2001) Hannoun, Nisreen, "Arab women connect: By, for and about Arab women," *infoDev*, 15 April 2001, http://www.iicd.org/base/story_ read_all?id=95 (18 August 2002).

(Harvard, 2002) *URLs Blocked in Saudi Arabia, Harvard Law School*, June 2002, http://cyber.law.harvard.edu/filtering/saudiarabia/saA.html (1 August 2002).

(Hassan, 2000) Hassan, Farkhonda, "Islamic women in science," *Science*, Vol. 290, No. 5489, 6 October 2000, http://www.sciencemag.org/cgi/content/full/290/5489/55 (26 August 2002).

(Hermida, 2002) Hermida, Alfred, "Saudis block 2,000 websites," BBC News, 31 July 2002, http://news.bbc.co.uk/1/hi/technology/2153312.stm (1 August 2002).

(Hudson, 2001) Hudson, Michael C., *Creative Destruction: Information Technology and the Political Culture Revolution in the Arab World*, revised version of a paper presented to the Conference on Trans-Nationalism, sponsored by the Royal Institute for Inter-Faith Studies, Amman, Jordan, June 19–21, 2001, http://nmit.georgetown.edu/papers/mchudson.htm (15 October 2001).

(Hunaidi, 2002) Hunaidi, Rima Khalaf, UNDP, United Nations, *Economic Development and Integration as a Catalyst for Peace*, in testimony before House International Relations Committee, 24 July 2002, Federal News Service, Inc., accessed through LexisNexis (20 August 2002).

(Hundley, n.d.) Hundley, Richard O., *Country Models of the Information Revolution: An Initial Set*, Santa Monica, Calif.: unpublished RAND research.

(Hundley et al., 2000) Hundley, Richard O., Robert H. Anderson, Tora K. Bikson, James A. Dewar, Jerrold D. Green, Martin C. Libicki, and C. Richard Neu, *The Global Course of the Information Revolution: Political, Economic, and Social Consequences:*

Proceedings of an International Conference, Santa Monica, Calif.: RAND, CF-154-NIC, 2000.

(Hundley et al., 2001)   Hundley, Richard O., Robert H. Anderson, Tora K. Bikson, Maarten Boterman, Jonathan A. Cave, C. Richard Neu, Michelle Norgate, and Renée Cordes, *The Future of the Information Revolution in Europe: Proceedings of an International Conference*, Santa Monica, Calif.: RAND, CF-172-NIC, 2001.

(InfoDev, 2002)   Information for Development Program (infoDev), *Quarterly Report*, First Quarter 2002, http://www.infodev.org/library/QR/qr102.pdf (18 August 2002).

([Int@j], 2002)   Information Technology Association Jordan, "Jordan Telecom to Hold Convergence 2002 in July," Int@j, July 2002, http://www.intaj.net/news/readnews.cfm?id=477 (31 July 2002).

(IRNA, 2002)   "Malaysian company host of website used by Al-Qaeda movement," Islamic Republic of Iran News Agency, 9 July 2002, http://www.irna.com/en/world/020709093712.ewo.shtml (10 July 2002).

(ITP, 2002a)   International Technology Publishing, "KSA tops Middle East nations in readiness for e-government," ITPnet, 4 June 2002a, http://www.itp.net/news/102319312245573.htm (4 June 2002a).

(ITP, 2002b)   International Technology Publishing, "Hajj pilgrimage to benefit from internet technology," ITPnet, 4 June 2002b, http://www. itp.net/news/102319673443134.htm (4 June 2002b).

(ITU, 2000)   International Telecommunication Union, *Arab States Telecommunication Indicators 2000*, April 2000, http://www.itu.int/ITU-D/ict/ statistics/at_glance/ARTI00_E.pdf (28 July 2002).

(ITU, 2001)   ITU Bureau of Telecommunication Development, *ITU Telecommunication Indicators Update: January–February–March 2001*, March 2002, http://www.itu.int/ITU-D/ict/update/pdf/Update_1_01.pdf (28 July 2002).

(ITU, 2002a)   ITU Strategy and Policy Unit, *Policy and Strategy Trends: January–February–March 2002*, June 2002a, http://www.itu.int/osg/spu/spunews/jan-march/jan-marchtrends.pdf (28 July 2002a).

(ITU, 2002b)   ITU Strategy and Policy Unit, *Policy and Strategy Trends: April–May–June 2002*, June 2002b, http://www.itu.int/osg/spu/spunews/apr-jun/Trends_062E.pdf (28 July 2002b).

(Joha, 2002) Joha, Ghassan, "Radio Sawa: Propaganda by any other name?" *The Star* (Amman), 17 August 2002, http://star.arabia.com/article/0,5596, 187_5436,00.html (15 September 2002).

(Kabege, 2002)   Kabege, Juliet, "Nile perch—Information at the source of the river Nile; Lake Victoria," infoDev, 15 April 2002, http://www.iicd.org/base/story/story_read_all?id=4947 (18 August 2002).

(Kamili, 2002) Kamili, Abdel Qader, *New Media and Change in the Arab World*, paper presented at the New Media and Change in the Arab World conference, Amman, Jordan, 28 February 2002, http://www.media-arabia.org/userfiles/Kamili.doc (20 August 2002).

(Kashkoul, 2002) Kashkoul, Nabil M., and Molouk Y. Ba-Isa, "Toward the ICT revolution," *Arab News*, 26 May 2002, http://www.arabnews.com/Top100/ toward_the_ict_revolution.htm (4 August 2002).

(Kedzie, 1997) Kedzie, Christopher R., *Communication and Democracy: Coincident Revolutions and the Emergent Dictator's Dilemma*, Ph.D. dissertation, Santa Monica, Calif.: RAND RSGD-127, 1997, http://www.rand.org/publications/RGSD/RGSD127/sec2.html (18 August 2002).

(Kelley, 2002) Kelley, Jack, "Militants wire Web with links to jihad," *USA Today*, 9 July 2002, http://www.usatoday.com/life/cyber/tech/2002/07/10/terrorweb.htm (10 July 2002).

(Kelly, et al., 2001) Kelly, Tim, Guy Girardet, and Magda Ismail, *Internet on the Nile: Egypt Case Study*, International Telecommunications Union, March 2001.

(Khiyami, 1994) Khiyami, Sami, Professor, University of Damascus, Electrical Engineering Faculty, *Information Technology Policies and Computerization Guidelines in a Third World Environment*, paper presented at the First Al-Shaam International Conference on Information Technology, Damascus, Syria, 9 May 1994.

(Knights, 2001) Knights, Michael, "Gulf censors try to keep up," *Jane's Intelligence Review*, 19 October 2001, http://jir.janes.com/subscribe/ international/jir1603.html (25 October 2001).

(LaMotte, 2002) LaMotte, Greg, "UN: Digital divide in Arab world 'staggering,'" *VOA News* (Cairo), 27 June 2002.

(Lee, 2001) Lee, Jennifer, "Companies compete to provide Saudi Internet veil," *The New York Times*, 19 November 2001, http://www.nytimes.com/2001/11/19/technology/19SAUD.html (19 November 2001).

(Lendenmann and Renfro, 2002) Lendenmann, Neal, and Rob Renfro, "Re-defining societal roles and professionalism: International Arab women in media conference," *GulfWire Perspectives*, 1 April 2002, http://www.arabialink.com/GulfWire/PerspArchives2002/GWP_2002_04_01.htm (12 July 2002).

(Mahmud, 2002) Mahmud, Abdel Aziz, *The Arab World and the Internet*, paper presented at the New Media and Change in the Arab World conference, Amman, Jordan, 28 February 2002, http://www.media-arabia.org/userfiles/abdul%20aziz%20-%20E%20-%20Final.doc (20 August 2002).

(Maurice, 2002) Maurice, Magda, *The Arab Viewer and Media Revolution*, paper presented at the New Media and Change in the Arab World conference, Amman, Jordan, 27 February 2002, http://www.media-arabia.org/userfiles/Madga%20Maurice-E.doc (20 August 2002).

(Meyer, 2000) Meyer, Chris, "'What's the matter?' New rule 1 in '10 driving principles of the new economy,'" *Business 2.0*, March 2000.

(Mulhem, 2002) Mulhem, Nabil, *Analysis on Satellite Viewers in Syria*, paper presented at the New Media and Change in the Arab World conference, Amman, Jordan, 27 February 2002, http://www.media-arabia.org/userfiles/ACF8CF1.doc (20 August 2002).

(Mustafa, 2002a) Mustafa, Ahmed, *Role of New Media in Economic Change in the Arab World*, paper presented at the New Media and

Change in the Arab World conference, Amman, Jordan, 1 March 2002a, http://www.media-arabia.org/userfiles/ACF2D99.doc (20 August 2002a).

(Mustafa, 2002b) Mustafa, Ahmed, "Media business in Arab states growing," *Gulf News* (Dubai, UAE), 31 March 2002b.

(Nair, 2002) Nair, Manoj, "Growth in Web users declines," *Gulf News* (Dubai) online edition, 7 August 2002, http://www.gulfnews.com/Articles/News.asp?ArticleID=59967 (12 August 2002).

(Nayyer, 2002) Nayyer, Kim, "Globalization of information: Intellectual property law implications," *First Monday*, Vol. 7, No. 1 (January 2002), http://firstmonday.org/issues/issue7_1/nayyer/index.html (4 August 2002).

(NIC, 2000) National Intelligence Council, *Global Trends 2015: A Dialogue About the Future with Nongovernment Experts*, NIC 2000–02, December 2000.

(Nielsen, 2002) "Worldwide Internet population grows slightly," *Nielsen NetRatings*, 16 August 2002, http://www.nua.ie/surveys/index.cgi?f=VS &art_id=905358274&rel=true (20 August 2002).

(Niewiaroski, 2002) Niewiaroski, Donald H., Jr., "Arab IT sector forecast continued growth," *U.S.-Arab Tradeline*, 5 April 2002, http://www.arabdatanet.com/news/DocResults.asp?DocId=3291 (25 July 2002).

(Norton, 2001) Norton, Lucy, *The Expanding Universe: Internet Adoption in the Arab Region*, World Markets Research Center, December 2001, http://www.worldmarketsanalysis.com/InFocus 2002/articles/middleeast_internet.html (25 July 2002).

(Nua, 2002a) "Global Internet audience increases," Nua.com, 13 August 2002a, http://www.nua.ie/surveys/index.cgi?f=VS&art_id=905358259&rel=true (20 August 2002a).

(Nua, 2002b) "Number of Internet cafes in UAE doubles," Nua.com, 14 August 2002b, http://www.nua.ie/surveys/index.cgi?f=VS&art_id= 905358264&rel=true (20 August 2002b).

(Obeidat, 2002) Obeidat, Reem Jamal, *Electronic Government: Aims and Pivots (The Case of the Dubai Experiment)*, paper presented at the New Media and Change in the Arab World conference, Amman, Jordan, 28 February 2002, http://www.media-arabia.org/userfiles/Obeidat-E-Government-E.doc (20 August 2002).

(Pacific Council, 2002)   Pacific Council on International Policy, *Roadmap for E-Government in the Developing World*, Los Angeles: The Working Group on E-Government in the Developing World, April 2002, http://www.accenture.com/xd/xd.asp?it=enweb&xd=newsroom/epresskit/egov/epres_realizing.xml (27 July 2002).

(Paltridge, 2001) Paltridge, Sam, "Local access pricing and the international digital divide," *On the Internet*, September 2001, http://www.isoc.org/oti/articles/1000/paltridge.html (8 August 2002).

(Perlez, 2002)   Perlez, Jane, "U.S. trying to market itself to young, suspicious Arabs," *The New York Times*, 14 September 2002, http://www.nytimes.com/2002/09/16/international/middleeast/1 6ARAB.html (15 September 2002).

(Public Voice, 2001) "The public voice and the digital divide: A report to the DOT force," *The Public Voice*, March 2001, http://www.thepublic voice.org/dotforce/DOT_Force_Report.pdf (27 July 2002).

(Qadhi, 2002) Qadhi, Mohammad, *Main Constraints of Media Drive in Yemen*, paper presented at the New Media and Change in the Arab World conference, Amman, Jordan, 27 February 2002, http://www.media-arabia.org/userfiles/ACFD4AA.doc (20 August 2002).

(Reuters, 2002) "U.S. to spread message through global comms office," *Reuters*, 30 July 2002, http://www.signonsandiego.com/news/nation/terror/20020730-0716-bush-image.html (15 September 2002).

(RSF, 2002) Reporters Sans Frontiéres (RSF), *Enemies of the Internet*, undated, http://www.rsf.org/ennemis.php3 (27 July 2002).

(Said, 2000) Said, Nabil, "The story of a new IT generation in Egypt," infoDev, 31 August 2000, http://www.iicd.org/base/story_read_all?id= 4377 (18 August 2002).

(Sawalha, 2001) Sawalha, Francesca, "Progress with IT not as fast as leadership, private sector wish, but outlook remains positive," *Jordan Times* (Amman), 8 December 2001.

(Sawalha, 2002) Sawalha, Francesca, "REACH 3.0 to be launched on Saturday," *Jordan Times* (Amman), 27 June 2002, http://www.jordanembassyus.org/06272002007.htm (31 July 2002).

(Seybold, 2000) Seybold, Patricia B., "'Ubiquity breeds wealth,' new rule 6 in '10 driving principles of the new economy,'" *Business 2.0*, March 2000.

(Simon, 2001) Simon, Leslie David, "New media and the Middle East: The impact of the Internet and satellite TV," presentation in *The Middle East Project and Sovereignty in the Digital Age* series, Woodrow Wilson International Center for Scholars, 24 September 2001.

(Symon, 2002) Symon, Fiona, "UN report criticises Arab states," BBC, 2 July 2002, http://news.bbc.co.uk/1/hi/world/middle_east/2082872.stm (4 August 2002).

(Taweela, 2002) Taweela, Waheed, *New Media in the Arab World: The Social and Cultural Aspect*, paper presented at the New Media and Change in the Arab World conference, Amman, Jordan, 1 March 2002, http://www.media-arabia.org/userfiles/ACF8DF0.doc (20 August 2002).

(Teitelbaum, 2002) Teitelbaum, Joshua, "Dueling for *Da'wa*: State vs. society on the Saudi Internet," *Middle East Journal*, Vol. 56, No. 2, Spring 2002, http://www.al-bab.com/media/docs/saudi.htm (2 June 2002).

(Treverton and Mizell, 2001) Treverton, Gregory F., and Lee Mizell, *The Future of the Information Revolution in Latin America: Proceedings of an International Conference*, Santa Monica, Calif.: RAND, CF-166-1-NIC, 2001.

(UNDP, 2000) *Gender Programmes: Regional Bureau for Arab States (RBAS)*, United Nations Development Programme, 10 October 2000, http://www.undp.org/gender/about/rbas_programmes. html#stats (26 August 2002).

(UNDP, 2001) United Nations Development Programme, "Today's technological transformations—creating the network age," *Human Development Report 2001*, Chapter 2, 2001, http://www. undp.org/hdr2001/complete.pdf (14 July 2002).

(UNDP, 2002) United Nations Development Programme, *Arab Human Development Report 2002: Creating Opportunities for Future Generations*, 2 July 2002, http://www.undp.org/rbas/ahdr/ CompleteEnglish.pdf (26 August 2002).

(UNIFEM, 1995) United Nations Development Fund for Women, *Plenary Address to the Fourth World Conference on Women*, 1995, http://www.unifem.org. jo/economic_empowerment.htm#profile (20 August 2002).

(Ved, 2002) Ved, Sima, "Women power: Talent to succeed," *Gulf News*, Online Edition (Dubai), http://www.gulfnews.com/Articles/ people-places.asp? ArticleID=59542 (4 August 2002).

(WomenWatch, 2002) United Nations Department of Economic and Social Affairs, *Information and Communication Technologies and Their Impact on and Use as an Instrument for the Advancement and Empowerment of Women*, online discussion, 17 June to 19 July 2002, http://www.un.org/womenwatch/daw/egm/ict2002/online. html.